Hagit Lavsky
The Creation of the German-Jewish Diaspora

Hagit Lavsky

The Creation of the German-Jewish Diaspora

—

Interwar German-Jewish Immigration to Palestine, the USA, and England

DE GRUYTER
OLDENBOURG   **MAGNES**

ISBN 978-3-11-063430-3
e-ISBN (PDF) 978-3-11-050165-0
e-ISBN (EPUB) 978-3-11-049809-7

Library of Congress Cataloging-in-Publication Data
A CIP catalog record for this book has been applied for at the Library of Congress.

Bibliographic information published by the Deutsche Nationalbibliothek
The Deutsche Nationalbibliothek lists this publication in the Deutsche Nationalbibliografie;
detailed bibliographic data are available on the Internet at http://dnb.dnb.de.

© 2018 Walter de Gruyter GmbH, Berlin/Boston
& Hebrew University Magnes Press, Jerusalem
This volume is text- and page-identical with the hardback published in 2017.
Cover illustration: bpk
Typesetting: Konvertus
Printing and binding: CPI books GmbH, Leck

♾ Printed on acid-free paper
Printed by Germany

www.degruyter.com
www.magnespress.co.il

Table of Contents

List of Figures, Tables and Graphs

Figures

DOI 10.1515/9783110501650-202

Tables

Graphs

Preface

The present book is the product of long time research, conducted with intervals over the last decade and a half. Throughout these years I was fortunate to be assisted by various grants and research institutions as follows:

Israel Foundation Trustees, research grant for project on interwar Jewish migration (with Prof. J. Metzer of The Hebrew University of Jerusalem), 2002–2004; Israel Science Foundation, research grant for project on the Jewish immigration to Palestine during the 1920th (with Prof. J. Metzer of The Hebrew University of Jerusalem); The Matthew Family Fellowship at the Center for Advanced Holocaust Studies, the United States Holocaust Memorial Museum, Washington, D.C, 2005; The Phyllis Greenberg Heideman and Richard D. Heideman Fellowship at the Center for Advanced Holocaust Studies, the United States Holocaust Memorial Museum, Washington, D.C., 2007.

Over the years I spent periods of sabbaticals at the the Skirball Department of Hebrew and Judaic Studies, New York University (1999, 2002); the Department of Hebrew and Jewish Studies, University College London, (1999, 2002); The Department of History (2008) and the Younes and Soraya Nazarian Center for Israel Studies (2011), both at the University of California Los Angeles (UCLA). These sabbaticals opened a whole range of opportunities to make use of treasures – archives and libraries – located in Britain and the United States beyond those situated in Israel. Thus I benefited from the good advice and generous assistance of librarians and archivists of the following institutions: The Oral History Division, the Institute of Contemporary Jewry, the Hebrew University of Jerusalem; the Central Zionist Archives, Jerusalem; Yad Vashem Research Center; The Wiener Library, London; The Mocatta Library, London; The Imperial War Museum, London; The British Library, London; the Library of Congress, Washington, D.C.; the Center for Advanced Holocaust Studies, USHMM, Washington, D.C.; Leo Baeck Institute Archives, and the YIVO Archives, both of them at the Center for Jewish History, New York.

I am grateful to countless colleagues and students beyond my ability to name them all, whose wise advice, comments and questions helped to consolidate this study. I would like however to mention my two colleagues, Prof. Gur Alroey of the University of Haifa, and Prof. Guy Miron of the Open University of Israel, who read carefully the first draft and whose profound comments and suggestions, together with the remarks made by the anonymous reader on behalf of the Magnes Press, helped to improve and reshape the draft to its present form.

Last, but not least, my gratitude goes to the Director of the Magnes Press, Hai Tsabar, to the copy editor Joan Hooper, and above all to my editor at DeGruyter, Dr. Julia Brauch, together with other staff members, whose high level professional handling and friendly cooperation transformed the production process of the book into a joyful enterprise.

Special thanks go to the Central Zionist Archives, and the U.S. Holocaust Memorial Museum, for permitting the use of photos and reproducing them in short time and high quality, to the b p k Photo Agency for the picture on the cover, and to my friend Miryam Shomrat and her brother Gideon Sela for letting me the use of family pictures.

As always – without the constant loving support of my partner Natan Lavsky none of it would be possible.

This book is dedicated to the memory of my late parents, Meir Martin Plessner (1900–1973), and Eva Esther Plessner née Jeremias (1905–1991). Their life stories as German Zionists and immigrants to Israel inspired my research interests all along.

Kiryat Tivon, Israel, August 2016

Introduction

Comparative History of Jewish Migration

In his conclusion to the book *Branching Out: German-Jewish Immigration to the United States, 1820–1914*,[1] historian Avraham Barkai compares the profile of the German-Jewish immigrants in America to the Jewish population remaining in Germany. He finds great similarity between patterns of social, political and economic behavior of the two communities, despite the change in environment and context. He claims, in addition, that German Jews – more than other migrant minorities – maintained their distinctive character, adding that further comparative studies are needed.

Barkai's observations did not emerge from an unexplored field. As an economic historian he had already been part of the newest trend in that historical discipline. During the last three or more decades historiography has expanded its horizon by paying more and more attention to social and cultural issues, to "history from below" and adopted question-sets and tools derived from the social sciences. One of the crucial sets of questions and methodologies that received an impetus from the social-science oriented approach is that of comparative analysis. Indeed, the historian – by definition – is interested in telling a story, a story whose components are unique in that they occurred in their composition only once in place and time. In contrast, the social scientist focuses on selected patterns in human behavior in similar contexts and tries to derive a model applicable to many historical sets in various times and places. The comparison breaks continuities, cuts through entanglements, and interrupts the flow of narration. Moreover, comparison implies selection, abstraction, and decontextualization to some degree. But the emphasis on context is dear and central to history as a discipline.[2] Indeed, there is a contradiction between telling a unique historical story and the comparative methodology that tends to emphasize similarities above the uniqueness of historical events that are crucial from the historical point of view.

One of the major fields of social-science oriented history is that of migration history, but comparative migration history is still young. A pioneering, and in a sense a model study of this kind has been presented by Samuel L. Baily.[3] In his study he suggests that a more nuanced investigation, regarding conditions in the origin country and differences between various groups of immigrants from

---

1 Barkai (1994).
2 Kocka (2003).
3 Baily (1999).

DOI 10.1515/9783110501650-001

the same origin country, combined with different circumstances in the destination countries produce different patterns of integration, adaptation and identity despite the common origin and culture. Baily has been followed by other migration historians, but hardly so by historians of Jewish migration.[4]

The research of Jewish migration has so far quite neglected the comparative approach. It has been concentrated primarily on the histories of the immigrating communities in their countries of destination– generally in isolation from each other.[5] This trend is partially connected with the still dominant assumption that Jewish migration was mainly refugee migration, the outcome of economic and political persecutions.[6] Historical research has only recently started to challenge this assumption.[7]

As a consequence, questions dominating social-science-based studies of migration movements – regarding conditions in countries of origin versus destinations, motives and considerations concerning migration and their effect on various migrating groups, choice of destinations, and how these differences in timing and choice affected immigrants' functioning within the various host societies – have thus hardly been asked.[8]

The study of Jewish immigration to Palestine (*aliya*) is an extreme example of this pattern. Conducted almost exclusively within the Zionist context it is based on the assumption that *aliya* – translated as ascent – was motivated by national ideology, and consequently unique in its social-demographic composition.[9] *Aliya* is mainly discussed from the perspective of its contribution to the development of the Jewish national entity in Palestine. This perspective has only seldom been challenged.[10]

Refuge, Immigration, *Aliya*

Contrary to the above mentioned currents, the hypothesis guiding this book is that Jewish migrations were not principally different from other mass migration movements, and were not necessarily refugee movements. Mass migrations were

---

4 One recent exception is Kobrin (2010), who focuses mainly on the diaspora-metropolitan interrelations and the construction of memory-community.

5 For example, Gartner (1960); Herscher (1982).

6 Marrus (2002).

7 Gartner (1998); Newman (1996); Sorin (1992).

8 The discussion on Jewish migration in Metzer (1998), 59–83, which uses a social science framework as an organizing theme, may be viewed as a recent exception to this pattern.

9 Eisenstadt (1954).

10 See Alroey (2002) and Metzer (1998), 59–83.

always a result of strong push factors combined with appealing pull factors. The most common push factor was the economic pressure that caused people to try their luck in those countries that offered opportunities to better their living conditions, and to prepare a better future for their offspring. From the subjective individual point of view, emigration is a drastic step that follows careful considerations of pros and cons. Against the hope for economic-social improvement, emigration entails uprooting from one's familiar cultural surroundings, separation from family members and friends, hardships in adjustment, courage to start anew in a strange foreign environment, and uncertainty regarding long-term eventual success. Therefore, even in cases of mass migration movements motivated by forceful economic push factors, often combined with political and social persecution that drove many to overcome the difficulties and to opt for emigration, as long as there were possibilities to arrive in another country, there were also the many people who did not embark on the big journey and stayed behind. To them the perils of emigration seemed more risky than the choice to continue life under economic, social, or political restrictions. The economic stand, moreover, of the persecuted group played a certain role when considering emigration. The wealthy could avoid persecution entirely or partially, while poverty prevented radical movement. Emigration could be an option only for those who had a certain degree of financial means or some connections abroad. The Jewish mass emigration from Russia from the 1870s until 1914 can serve as an illustration for mass migration that left millions of Jews behind.

What is then a refugee migration? The extreme definition would combine refuge with flight, namely the movement of people who are forced to leave under immediate threat to their lives, without having the possibility to consider if, when, and whereto. If there is no outlet, there are no possibilities to relocate – then the forced flight creates the problem of refugees, namely of people en masse trying desperately to leave their homeland, are unable to do so and as a consequence are under immediate danger.

From the international perspective, the modern problem of refugees became a dominant and constant problem particularly following World War I. Up until the war international migration was quite free and uncontrolled by state authorities, but following the war the issue of passports became mandatory and the control of borders more common. The new international system – the League of Nations – tried to cater for the various groups that found themselves forced to leave their home countries and instituted a High Commissioner for Refugees in 1935.[11] From then on, almost all who were under pressure to leave their countries were officially considered refugees.

---

11 Marrus (2002), 86–94.

Historically speaking there were many grey areas that exemplify the complexity of defining the issue of refugees as distinguished from the issue of immigrants. A compelling case is that of the thousand immigrants to the United States who were caught by the new quota law of 1921 (see Chapter 1) between Europe and the U.S. in various European ports, and became the concern of Jewish welfare organizations. Their predicament called into question the very meaning of immigrants. They were referred to in official records under an array of terms – refugees, transmigrants, emigrants, immigrants, stranded immigrants, and aliens.[12]

Nevertheless, the technical term of refugee should not be used as a working term applicable to the historiography of the entire post-World War I period. Many of those considered refugees under the auspices of the League of Nations or of welfare organizations were not really refugees from the point of view of the individuals under pressure.

This is true particularly for the German-Jewish interwar migration. Up until late 1938, emigration of the German Jew was rather an act of choice, even within the limited spectrum of possibilities and of growing limits posed by new immigration policies conducted by the optional destination countries. Therefore, in this study, in contrast to many studies, the German-Jewish migration up until late 1938 is not treated as a refugee migration, and motivations and choices of time and destination are carefully explored.

Another instrumental deviation from dominating scholarly trends that guides this study is that immigration to Palestine was not an exemption and cannot be explained on the basis of ideology per se. The individual Jew who acted under pressure of the push factor was considering his destination according to multiple considerations. Ideology might have been one component of his considerations, sometimes a strong component, but very rarely a decisive one, namely that would weigh against all contradicting factors. Therefore, until the mid-1920s, when Palestine could not be considered a feasible alternative, only a tiny trickle of immigrants came to Palestine. The vast interwar immigration waves that reached Palestine from then on are therefore treated here not differently from immigration to other countries.

To sum up this point – the present study deals with immigrants, and does not use either the term refugee or *aliya*, unless applicable to the usage at the time, or in the case of refugees as defined above.

---

12 Garland (2014), 68.

German-Jewish Interwar Migration: A View of the Research Terrain

The vast study concerning German-Jewish interwar migration has benefited from intensive research efforts, both contemporary and retrospective, driven largely by the deep impact that the unique circumstances of the refugee movement, resulting from the Nazis rise to power in Germany, had on contemporaries and historians. German Jewry excelled in the Jewish Diaspora in enjoying full emancipation and in its prominent cultural status and role in forming Germany as the center of modern culture in all fields of arts, humanities and sciences. The migration movement driven by the Nazis met with great shock because it was unprecedented. For many decades the mass migrations, both Jewish and non-Jewish, originated in eastern and southern Europe, in underdeveloped countries. This new mass migration was a movement of people who came from the most civilized modern country, had enjoyed prosperity and were well integrated into the general society. They were abruptly pushed out to face rigid immigration policies of potential destination countries, mostly affected by the economic depression. Their problem became a central issue on the international agenda. It was dealt with specific reference to the group's human capital, professionally and culturally, including an emphasis on leading figures in the world of arts and sciences. The uniqueness of this migration was seen differently from Palestinian, American and British perspectives. For the Jewish community in Palestine, just recovering from the economic depression of the second half of the 1920s, it was considered a great economic asset yet an unprecedented challenge. No wonder, therefore, that the German-Jewish immigration, which constituted only 20 percent of the large immigration wave of 1933–1939 (the Fifth *Aliya*), attracted much attention at the time, and thereafter.[13] Indeed, among the various groups of immigrants to Mandatory Palestine, the German group was examined far more than the much larger East European groups of immigrants.

In the U.S. and Britain, both under economic depression, immigration policy was hotly contested between those who favored the entrance of immigrants, accentuating the advantage of their human and financial capital, and those who feared the high percentage of professionals, whom the modern but stagnant economy could not absorb. Consequently, many studies were conducted to serve either argument in the debate.[14]

---

13 Britschgi-Schimmer (1936); Gelber (1990).
14 Angell and Buxton (1939); Davie and Koenig (1945).

Rather than the economic issue, it was the cultural aspect – the transfer of the centers of modern arts and sciences from Berlin and Vienna to New York, Los Angeles and London – which attracted contemporary attention and shaped the study onwards. Special arrangements were made, especially in Britain and the U.S., to make this transfer possible, and the Central European migration has been identified ever since with this cultural shift.[15] As a consequence, the historiography of German-Jewish interwar migration is characterized as follows:

A. The German-Jewish migration of the 1920s has hardly been dealt with.[16] The need to study it is particularly noticeable for Palestine and the U.S., the main destinations for Jewish emigrants from Weimar Germany who also played certain roles with regards to the later immigration of German Jews to those countries.

B. Most studies define the migration of the 1930s as refugee migration, barely referring to motives and considerations of the emigrants. Niederland has already proved that up to 1938, the potential emigrants did not consider themselves refugees. They considered possibilities, directions, and timing for emigration.[17]

C. "Regular" members of the migrating population have been largely neglected, despite the fact that they constituted the vast majority of the emigrants. Issues such as self-image and identity have been addressed, with only few exceptions, mainly with reference to writers and intellectuals who expressed their experiences in all kinds of publications or in private memoirs deposited in public archives[18] (it must be admitted though that they constituted a large number among the German emigrants).[19]

D. *Exilforschung*, or Refugee Studies, which focus on the intellectuals, scientists and artists expelled by the Nazi regime, has largely ignored the specific Jewish dimension. Stephanie Barron refers to it explicitly but briefly.[20] A few scholars, among them Michael Meyer, Guy Miron and Daniel Snowman, focus on the Jewish aspect of the exiles.[21]

---

15 To mention only few examples: Heilbut (1997); Coser (1984); Jay (1986); Berghaus (1989).

16 Niederland's study is an exception, which highlights the need for further research: Niederland (1996). See also: Stone (1997).

17 Niederland (1996). See also Pross (1955).

18 A collection of some 1,000 memoirs is located at the Leo Baeck Institute in New York (LBINY).

19 A few studies were devoted to the rank and file migrants: Benz (1991); Loewenstein (1989); Miron (2005).

20 Barron and Eckmann (1997), 23.

21 Meyer (2001); Miron (2005); Snowman (2002). A recent study may be mentioned here as well: Aschheim (2007).

E. Concentrating on the intellectual and cultural transfer meant naturally dealing with "Central European" emigration in general. No distinction was made in the research literature between the three groups of German-speaking migrants – Germans, Austrians and Czechs. Distinctive political, social, economic and cultural backgrounds and profiles, norms of behavior and social conduct of each group have seldom been touched upon. Therefore, many questions have not been asked, such as: How did these differences affect the timing and directions of emigration? Had they influenced distinctive patterns of adjustment? To what extent did these groups merge with each other in their host countries?

This overview clearly demonstrates that there is still a need for a systematic study focusing on German Jewry, comparatively examining the German-Jewish immigration in the various countries.[22]

This book is meant to fill the gap in the history of Jewish migration in general, and that of the German-Jewish migration in particular, by applying a comparative perspective, by relating to the individual rank-and-file immigrants and their choices as historical subjects, and by focusing on the German group alone, without mixing it with other German-speaking groups of immigrants.

Despite the seemingly common background of the German-Jewish emigrants, their motivation to emigrate was affected by various factors related to timing and choice of destinations, and resulting in distinct socio-economic characteristics of the immigrants in the different destinations. A comparative study of the different routes of the emigrating German Jews should be able to trace the similarities and differences in their profiles, patterns of adjustment, the role they played in the host countries, and the extent to which they preserved a common character as German Jews. Concentrating on the Jews emigrating from Germany to their three major overseas destination countries also opens the possibility to trace the combined impacts of immigrant profiles and of the circumstances within the receiving countries in different times in shaping the distinct characteristics of each group, the different patterns of absorption and adjustment, and the role and function of each group in its new country and society.

This comparative study of seemingly one segment of the Jewish people – German Jewry – connects with the recent trend to view Jewish history across borders,[23] and at the same time reveals the distinction of the German-Jewish

---

22 An example for such a comparative study in a different context is Gur Alroey's pioneering work, comparing the pre-WWI Russian Jewish immigrants to Palestine with those who immigrated to the U.S.: Alroey (2004).
23 Rosman (2009).

identity when encountering different societies. The story of the interwar German-Jewish emigration is a nuanced story dispersed through different routes and destinations. To the challenge posed by Avraham Barkai's hypothesis regarding the common uniqueness of German-Jewish immigrants that opened this introduction, this study presents an alternative historical perspective and brings to the forefront the question: Did German-Jewish migration really created a distinctive German-Jewish Diaspora or did it put an end to the German chapter in Jewish history? Is it true that the mass emigration and murderous annihilation put an end to German Jewry in Germany, but created a German-Jewish Diaspora instead? This book offers some insights and different perspectives to deal with this question.

Chapter 1
History and Memory

In May 2004 an international conference took place in Mishkenot Sha'ananim, Jerusalem. Under the title "The Yekkes" (nickname used in Israel in reference to Jews of German origin), this conference was dedicated to the legacy of German Jews in Israel. The organizers had not anticipated the wide reverberations this conference would have among the older German-Jewish immigrants and their off-spring. Hundreds of them, with their children and grandchildren, descendants of the wide German-speaking population in Israel, showed up to declare in public their German affiliation and to enjoy the recognition and reputation of their significance in Israel that this conference indeed expressed. Many of them could not find seats in the large conference hall; elderly men sat on the steps, others gathered in adjacent rooms with closed circuit television. Indeed, many expressed their anger regarding the organizers, and endeavored to discipline – quite typical for Yekkes – those who tried to squeeze themselves to the head of the queue.

The lectures delivered in this conference were published a year later.[1] The title of the collection is a citation from the poem "Oren" (Pine Tree) by Lea Goldberg, which appears on the front page:

> Perhaps only the wandering birds
> While hanging between earth and sky
> Do know this pain of two homelands[2]

Both the title of the conference and that of the volume share the feeling of uniqueness and incomplete integration of the immigrants in Israel, but differ in perspective. The conference title meant to emphasize the cultural significance of the German sector within the broad Israeli culture as viewed by others – negatively or positively – and expressed by the term "Yekkes." The book's title, however, transmits the editors' perception that the German immigrants (like other immigrants, indeed, Goldberg refers to homelands other than Germany) never abandoned their loving connection with their German homeland, and never completely integrated in their new homeland, Israel. Indeed, the volume's various parts reflect both approaches. On the one hand, the first part is titled "German-Jewish

---

1 Zimmermann and Hotam, eds (2006).

2 אוּלַי רַק צִפֳּרֵי-מַסָּע יוֹדְעוֹת –
כְּשֶׁהֵן תְּלוּיוֹת בֵּין אֶרֶץ וְשָׁמַיִם –
אֶת זֶה הַכְּאֵב שֶׁל שְׁתֵּי הַמּוֹלָדוֹת.
(translated by the author – H. L.)

DOI 10.1515/9783110501650-002

identity" and is dedicated to the baggage brought from there, from Germany, but the majority of the articles appear under the two following parts (German-Jewish identity in migration; The realms of Yekkes' memory) are dedicated to the contribution of German immigrants to the cultural modernization in Israel, in the fields of art, theater, music, sports, the media, economics, and even in the realm of political diplomacy, and many more.

Until the 1990s, the epithet "Yekke" was used to express disrespect. It was meant to characterize the German Jews as totally different from the Eastern European Jews, as being restrained, square, pedant, arrogant and alienated. The source for this nickname is not clear. Some argue that it derives from the word *Jacke* in German (pronounced yakke), which means jacket, since the Yekkes always wore them with a tie despite the country's summer heat. Others jokingly explain that the term is an acronym for *yehudi keshe havana* (slow-witted Jew). This epithet circulated only in Israel and not in other German-Jewish locales. This manifestation alludes to the unparalleled self-awareness of the immigrants from Germany. Yekke was directed exclusively to those who came from Germany, and not to any other German-speaking immigrant who originated in former regions of the Austro-Hungarian Empire whose everyday culture differed from that of the Germans, and who did not shoulder the baggage of mutual antipathy toward Eastern European Jews, the "*Ost-juden.*" The children of Yekkes did whatever they could to hide their origin and to wipe out any sign in their norms and manners that could identify them with what they considered to be the shameful alienation of their parents.[3] Now, all of a sudden, the conference manifested that the Yekkes began to take pride of their title, and, moreover, descendants of German-speaking parents streamed to the conference, eager to be included among the Yekkes, to wear the title as a token of honor, apparently to declare – "we are not ashamed anymore but proud to be Yekkes, we enjoy its positive recognition and wish to continue to bear it gloriously into the future."

The conference was the most outstanding in a series of expressions of this new pride pronounced by members of the second generation with the wish to promote recognition of their parents' legacy as German Jews and their contribution to the building of the Jewish state, and to follow in their footsteps by implementing their cultural and social norms in Israeli society. The first event in this series was an exhibition on the German immigrants, inaugurated in 1993 to mark the 60th anniversary of the Central European immigration in the Fifth *Aliya*. The exhibition travelled between the three main cities – Tel Aviv, Jerusalem, and Haifa – accompanied by an illustrated catalogue.[4] The titles in the catalogue

---

3 Based on my personal experience and observations.
4 Goldfein (1993).

testify to the spirit of the exhibition: Almost 30 percent turned to agriculture; Youth *Aliya* – a rescue and educational enterprise; Innovative initiative: the middle-class agricultural settlements; Nahariya – the pioneer of Western Galilee; New impetus of industrial development; Guesthouses and hotels; Reinvigoration of the health system; Pioneers of the welfare system; A place of honor in the judicial system; In all fields of academic research – a crucial contribution to the development of the *Yishuv* (the Palestine Jewish community); Outstanding intellectuals and educators; Central European immigrants in the Israeli media; The Yekkes in the arts; Prosperity in musical life; Volunteering for security services; In the service of state and society; In the diplomatic service. Only one title indicated the limits of pride: In politics – limited impact. Many observers were annoyed by the avoidance of many more areas of Yekke imprint, such as their share in the *Kibbutz* movement in general, and that of the religious *Kibbutz* in particular.

A decade later, in 2003, a new initiative appeared, the journal *Yakinton* (Hyacinth, the Hebrew term alludes to Yekke) of the Association of Israelis of Central European Origin (*Yakinton: Mitteilungsblatt* (MB) *der Vereinigung der Israelis Mitteleuropäischer Herkunft.* Hebrew: Irgun Yots'ei Merkaz Eropa). The greater part of the journal appears in Hebrew, but it also includes a German section. The founding editor was the journalist Micha Limor, a second generation descendent. It appears approximately every two months, and its issues include articles, memories, book reviews and testimonies mainly relating to the important contribution of the Yekkes to the country.

The journal reflects the dominating aspiration of the Association of Israelis of Central European Origin, headed by Reuven Merhav (also second generation) to bequeath the German-Jewish legacy to Israeli society. The Association launched a website, much of which aimed at documenting the German-Jewish imprint in Israel. One of many projects is the "Yekkes book" meant to collect, preserve and perpetuate the contribution of the Yekkes to the building and development of Israel.[5] Other projects of the Association include the Museum at Tefen, originally established in 2004 by the industrialist Stef Wertheimer, which presents the activities and impact of the Yekkes and the German-Jewish culture on Israeli society. The Association also developed an educational program for teachers and instructors, focusing on German-Jewish legacy's social and moral values relevant for implementation today: mutual responsibility, aspiration for excellence, education, public service based on proper, honest and transparent management, tolerance, and the acceptation of the Other.

---

5 *Irgun Yotsei Merkaz Eropa:*http://www.irgun-jeckes.org *(last accessed 30 December, 2014).* Merhav has just retired in September 2016.

All these initiatives signify the effort made by the second and third generations to reassure that the German immigration was a significant contribution to the Zionist epopee of building the national home, not less than their predecessors, the acclaimed pioneers of former immigration waves, in particular the Second *Aliya* (1904–1914) and the Third *Aliya* (1919–1923) from Russia. To regain Zionist dignity has become the basis for the on-going project to construct the Central European legacy as an indispensable asset for the present Israeli society. The publication of German-Jewish immigrant reminiscences opens their stories to the wider public and might compensate for past contempt and properly integrate their special individual and communal stories within the fabric of Israeli self-awareness. This trend is not unique to the Central European case in Israel, and exists in a variety of Israeli immigrant societies in the era of privatization and pluralism. What is special in the German-Jewish case is that the intention is not to repair and compensate for discrimination by the veteran elite, but to demand the integration of the German story within the heroic national narrative, to emphasize its importance in the Zionist epic and promote its potential for the general society, present and future.

The American and the British scenarios are totally different. In America it is difficult to find any obvious sign of German-Jewish identity. Indeed, the German-Jewish newspaper, *Aufbau*, established in 1934, continued to appear until 2004, but its distribution was extremely limited. Public events concerning the German-Jewish immigrants are rare. In 2004/5 the Jewish Museum in Baltimore displayed an exhibition documenting the history of the German refugees in that city.[6] The Leo Baeck Institute in New York occasionally presents exhibitions or lectures concerning German-Jewish culture in general, not necessarily in connection with the German-Jewish immigration and life in the U.S.A. Groups that emphasize self-identity are limited to small circles, such as the *Stammtisch* (German for "regulars' table," an informal group meeting held on a regular basis) in New York where old German Jews meet with young Germans who are allowed to substitute their military service for national service aimed at supporting elderly Holocaust survivors; or the circle of Central-Europeans in Los Angeles.[7] Other than these small contributions there are no visible efforts to emphasize or to foster accounts of the German-Jewish element as a unique component within pluralistic American society,[8] except for books and exhibitions dedicated to the intellectual and

---

6 *Lives Lost* (2004).

7 Based on my personal acquaintance with the *Stammtisch* in New York. See also Wolman (1996).

8 Based on personal experience and on a survey through the *Aufbau* issues http://deposit.ddb.de/online/exil/exil.htm

artistic contribution of refugees from Nazi Germany to the American cultural and academic scene.[9]

The British situation is different. Here it is possible to see the intensive activity that documented and propagated information about the saga of German-Jewish refugees and their absorption and integration. In 2002 the Association of Jewish Refugees (AJR) presented an exhibition titled "Continental Britons," based on 150 video interviews with Central Europeans who told their stories of immigration and integration. The exhibition, along with accompanying lectures and discussions, transmitted the following message clearly: "We came here as refugees, we have experienced all sort of difficulties getting out from Germany and getting settled in Britain, and we are grateful to the English people who welcomed us despite the difficulties and we are happy to have become British, although we admit that our origins and culture are quite part of us and noticeable to others."[10]

In Britain, like in Israel, the German-Jewish organizations are actively documenting their immigration and settlement experiences, but the messages of their endeavors are extremely different. In Israel they strive to integrate their story into the national epic and to highlight their extraordinary contribution in the past and its potential contribution for the future. In Britain the message is the recognition of the British generosity and the gratefulness of refugees who will never forget their being refugees despite the success of integration.

Although there was much in common in the cultural and social character of the immigrants from Germany and much in common in their experiences in their various destinations, the different timings and circumstances of their emigration and of the social, cultural, economic and political situations at their destinations were more significant in creating the differences between these three German-Jewish Diasporas. Israel and Britain represent the two opposing poles on the absorption axis: the one is the outcome of self-perception of superiority and pride mixed with a sort of disappointment and drive for correction; the other is the outcome of refugee complex that is there to stay. The American case stands in between – no superiority and no complex. It is almost a disappearing historical chapter in the American-Jewish narrative. The different ways in constructing collective memory and in *Landsmannschaft* activity are directly connected with the processes of immigration and integration in the three destinations of the interwar German-Jewish migration, discussed in the following chapters

---

9 Barron and Eckmann (1997).

10 Based on personal acquaintance with the interviewer and the exhibition curator, Dr. Bea Levkovitz; Refugee Voices, WLL London; and on attending the exhibition and the lectures. The exhibition is presented on the website of AJR: http://www.ajr.org.uk

Chapter 2
Interwar Overseas Jewish Migration: An Overview

Changing Origins and Refugee Movements

World War I was a major turning point in the history of Jewish migration movement. The prewar era was marked by Jewish mass overseas immigration from
Eastern Europe to the West. Within 40 years (1875–1914) about 2,200,000 Jews
immigrated to overseas destinations, of whom about two thirds – 1,300,000 –
went to the United States.[1]

The war hit the great Jewish settlement center in Eastern Europe directly and
hard. In 1915 and 1916, Russian military authorities drove tens of thousands of
Jews and German-speaking Protestants as potential collaborators into the inte-
rior of the country, German occupation troops conscripted thousands of Jews and
Poles as forced laborers, and in the Habsburg monarchy, a refugee wave to Vienna
and Budapest began after massive destruction in Galicia. Although the war ended
in the West in 1918, a series of armed conflicts began after the collapse of the mul-
tiethnic empires in Eastern Europe that would last into the early 1920s. Millions
of Eastern Europeans lost their homes, among them several hundred thousand
Jews. Large groups succeeded in fleeing to the West, but there most of them stood
before closed doors.[2]

The war interrupted the process of overseas migration for 68,000 immigrants,
and immediately after the war it seemed that the mass immigration, particularly
to the United States, was resumed, with 135,000 Jewish immigrants.[3] However,
fear of the spread of Bolshevism as well as explicit racist and anti-Semitic prej-
udices brought about a new restriction policy by the U.S.A. Other traditional
immigration countries such as Canada and Argentina also put up obstacles;
Britain didn't even bother to lift the mobility restrictions introduced during the
war. After 1917/1918, it was only possible to cross international borders with valid
passports. Many countries required visas and transit visas that often could only
be acquired with great difficulty. This proved particularly fateful for many citizens of the former Russian and Ottoman empires as well as the defunct Habsburg
monarchy. The governments of the successor states often refused to issue passports to members of undesirable minorities. Without papers, stateless individuals
lost their right to freedom of movement. Tens of thousands of Jews from Eastern

---

1 Lestchinsky (1944), 8; Alroey (2007), 65, 68.
2 Brinkmann (2010).
3 Alroey (2007), 68.

DOI 10.1515/9783110501650-003

Europe as well as Armenians and opponents of the Bolsheviks were in a state that is best described as permanent transit. Jewish refugees became stranded in refugee camps and inner city slums all over Europe. After 1939, many of these people fell into the clutches of the Nazi persecution machinery because they did not have valid identity and citizenship documents.

On the continent few countries were open to migrants from Eastern Europe after 1918. Apart from the Weimar Republic, which pursued a relatively liberal policy toward refugees, there was essentially France. In the Soviet Union, a strong Jewish country-to-town migration began. Many Jews were resettled in the East during the course of the Stalinist forced collectivization of the 1920s.[4]

Throughout Eastern Europe Jews were now on the move and represented a refugee crisis of major proportion. The League of Nations, still a fledgling institution, could not do much. Instead, about a dozen Jewish societies operated on an international level, including the *Alliance Israélite Universelle*, the Jewish Colonization Association (JCA, or ICA), the *Hilfsverein der Deutschen Juden*, and others. Among the most important were the American Jewish Joint Distribution Committee (Joint), and the newly founded (1921) United Committee of Jewish Emigration (Emigdirect). Facing the restrictions posed by the United States (to be dealt with hereafter) the Emigdirect cleared the way for overseas travel and explored alternative settlement possibilities, notably in South America, Canada, Australia, and South Africa. In 1927 it formed, together with the American-based Hebrew Sheltering and Immigrant Aid Society (HIAS) and ICA, the HICEM (taking its name from the initials of all three partners).[5]

The Great Depression that started in 1929 deprived numerous people of the financial means necessary for migration. Many countries, especially the United States, tightened their immigration restrictions further. This put great obstacles in the way of German-Jewish emigrants after Hitler's rise to power in 1933. The influx of immigrants from Germany into neighboring countries soon became a concern to the League of Nations which created a new office – a High Commissioner for Refugees, and appointed James G. McDonald of New York to the post.[6] Later, the Évian Conference in June 1938, which was called by the American president Franklin D. Roosevelt to discuss possibilities of facilitating the emigration of German and Austrian Jews, marked a low point. None of the 32 participating nations was willing to receive more than a few Jewish refugees. The threatening situation for Jews in Eastern Europe was not even a topic of the negotiations.

---

4 Alroey (2007).
5 Marrus (2002), 66–68.
6 Wischnitzer (1948), 182.

Many Eastern European states, especially Poland, pursued anti-Semitic policies in the mid-1930s and treated their Jewish citizens as de facto stateless.[7]

Limited Options and Changing Destinations

The war and its aftermath caused a radical change in the possibility of finding a destination overseas. Up until World War I, the two American continents absorbed over 90 percent of the total number of Jewish immigrants. After the war, the proportion of immigration to the Americas began to decrease.[8] The potential directions and destinations for those seeking to emigrate changed and narrowed due to the overall introduction of limiting immigration laws in many countries.

The following discussion will deal with the change focusing on the three countries whose role as destination altered dramatically and shaped the destiny of German-Jewish interwar out-of-Europe migration: U.S.A., Palestine under the British Mandate, and Britain.

The U.S. Immigration Policy

The U.S., which had received about two thirds of the mass European immigration prior to WWI, replaced its open door policy after the war with a restrictive quota system based on the country of origin and designed to prevent further change in the ethnic composition of the American population. The legal basis for immigration policy was defined by two acts. The first was the Regulating Immigration of Aliens of February 1917, which reflected U.S. concern regarding the large influx of Eastern Europeans, many of them illiterate, as well as "Asiatics" – the term used for Asians. The second was the Emergency Immigration Restriction Act of 1921, a stopgap until more encompassing legislation could be passed, reflected that fear. The recognition that more than 800,000 immigrants had been admitted to the United States during 1920–1921 illustrated the loose restrictions imposed by the immigration law of 1917. Of particular concern was the fear that many of these immigrants from Russia or Eastern Europe, many of them Jewish, were Bolsheviks or other kinds of radicals. The act limited the annual number of immigrants from each country to three percent of that nation's nationals present in the United States according to the 1910 U.S. Census. Total immigration was set at 357,803

---

7 Brinkman (2010).
8 Lestschinsky (1944), 7.

persons.[9] Nevertheless, under the 1921 temporary quota law and within the following three years, 1,539,371 immigrants, 153,232 of them Jews, were able to enter the United States legally.[10]

The immigration quotas were made permanent and considerably smaller in the Immigration Act of 1924 (the Johnson-Reed Act, or the National Origin Act). This act was intended to permanently restrict the immigration numbers from "undesirable" areas of the world – particularly from Russia and Eastern Europe. In addition to fears about radicalism, congressional leaders were concerned about the large influx of workers willing to work for substandard wages. The greatest influx of immigrants from Eastern and Southern Europe had occurred in the two to three decades prior to the start of World War I in 1914. Thus, the basis for the quota was changed from the U.S. Census of 1910 to that of 1890, when far fewer Southern and Eastern Europeans had resided in the United States. Furthermore, the quota was reduced from three to two percent of the number of foreign-born persons of each nationality resident in the United States in 1890. The legislation also defined who could enter as a "non-quota" immigrant. This category included wives and unmarried children (under 18 years of age) of U.S. citizens, residents of the West, religious or academic professionals, and "bona-fide students" under 15 years of age. Those not in any of these categories were referred to as "quota immigrants" and were subject to annual numerical limitations. For quota immigrants, the act stated that preference would be given to family members of U.S. citizens and to immigrants who were skilled in agriculture.

The quota provision did not however take effect until 1 July, 1929, on account of a difficulty of arriving at a definitive basis for determining national origins. After July 1927 permissible annual quotas for each nationality would be based on the national origins –"by birth or ancestry"– of the total U.S. population as recorded in 1920. According to the 1924 laws the total immigration quota was limited to 153,774 immigrants yearly; 31.9 percent of the yearly quota was allocated to the north-west European countries, of which Germany was allocated with 25,557 immigrants yearly. The quota policy involved obtaining a visa, which should prove that the holder fulfilled the requirements, in proving that he or she are not Likely to Become a Public Charge (LPC).

Thus, two new factors were specified in the 1924 act: the use of ethnicity as main criteria for establishing the quota assigned to national groups eligible for immigration; and – not less important – the provision that the visa-granting process would be subject solely to the judgment of the U.S. consuls abroad.[11]

---

9 Adler (2012); Zucker (2010).
10 Garland (2014), 68.
11 Zucker (2010).

In 1929, in response to the economic crisis, the law became more rigid in its visa-requirement provisions – that each applicant establish that it was not likely *or probable* that he or she would become a public charge, as distinguished from the previous formulation mentioning the mere possibility of becoming one. The American consuls who were in charge of granting the visas became actual "Gate Keepers" preventing immigration as much as possible.[12] As a consequence the consuls barred rather than opened the door for applicants following the Nazi seizure of power. There was an ever-growing gap, therefore, between the number of applicants and the number of visas granted, and the quota was never filled before 1938.

The U.S.A. had never distinguished between immigrants and refugees. However, in 1934 a distinction in favor of the refugees was incorporated in the law through regulations issued by the State Department, stating that consuls may waive the requirement with reference to documents not available where personal risk might ensue in obtaining such documents.[13] Moreover, in late 1938, following the *Anschluss* of Austria in March, the failure of the Evian Conference on refugees in July, and the *Kristallnacht* pogrom in November, the U.S. introduced more measures in order to address the refugee problem. These measures included mainly more flexibility in granting temporary permits for visitors, and in the handling of paper requirements by the consuls. However, the U.S. never abandoned the economic considerations guiding immigration policy, neither did it expand the quota nor alternately introduced a category of refugees to its immigration system. As a result, during the decade 1931–1940 only 580,000 immigrants entered the country, less than in any previous decade.[14]

Jewish Immigration to the U.S.A.

As a result of the post-WWI American immigration policy, the proportion of international migration that the U.S. was willing to take in declined and the number of Jews entering between 1920 and 1931 stood at 360,000 out of 733,000 total overseas Jewish migrants (see Table 1).[15]

The situation deteriorated particularly during the first years of the Nazi era, when only 14,000 (6 percent) of the Jewish emigrants from Europe entered the

12 Breitman and Kraut (1987), 7–10, 28–51; Marrus (1985), 137; Zucker (2001), 35–44; Zucker (2010).

13 Fields (1938), 10.

14 Daniels (1986).

15 These estimations do not reflect illegal immigration, dealt with in Garland (2014).

U.S.A. Towards the late 1930s, and particularly with the Americans alleviating some of the measures regarding refugees from Germany and Austria, the proportion of immigrants that the U.S. absorbed grew to 31 percent of the total Jewish migration.

On the whole, out of a total of 1,227,000 Jewish interwar overseas migrants only 37 percent were taken in by the U.S., notwithstanding the slight improvement during the late 1930s.

Table 1: Jewish interwar overseas migration

Period*	Total		Palestine		U.S.A.	
	thousands	%	thousands	% of total	thousands	% of total
1920–1931	733	100	115	16	360	49
1932–1935	249	100	161	65	14	6
1936–1939	246	100	86	35	81	31
1920–1939	1,227	100	362	29	455	37

* Periods dictated by the changes in the status op of Palestine as a destination vis-à-vis the U.S.A. Sources: Sicron (1957), Statistical Supplement, Tables A1, A5; Metzer (1998), 66: Table 3.1. Both sources include American data.

Palestine Immigration Policy

Parallel to the decline of the U.S. as the main destination, the post-World War I era was marked by the emergence of a new preferred destination for Jewish international migration, namely Palestine under the British Mandate, that provided a new framework for a Jewish national home.

The British Mandate of Palestine was a part of the new international system following WWI – the League of Nations and the Mandate system. It was unique among other mandates. Britain obtained the Mandate of Palestine with the provision to integrate the Balfour Declaration of 2 November, 1917, to assist the development of a Jewish national home. Consequently, the Palestine government opened the gates of Palestine, and introduced a liberal immigration policy aiming to attract immigrants and capital to help the process of modernization, conditioned by adjusting immigration to the economic absorption capacity of the country.

According to the Mandate draft confirmed and signed in 1923, the British rule had to some extent to cooperate with the Jewish Agency of Palestine (the Zionist Executive), that represented Jewish interests regarding the National Home. The issues of immigration and settlement were of first priority from the Jewish-Zionist point of view, and of primary concern for the Mandate Administration, which had to navigate between Jewish and Palestinian-Arab interests. The following discussion deals with the implications of immigration policies and practices as shaped and developed during the period under discussion rather than with the changed circumstances and British policies toward the National Home in general.

Under the British military occupation, until July 1920, immigration into Palestine was essentially free.[16] The first Immigration Ordinance was enacted in August 1920. Accordingly, the High Commissioner authorized the entrance of persons whose maintenance was to be guaranteed by the Zionist Organization for one year in addition to persons of independent means, and members of families of present residents.[17] The number of immigrants that the Zionist Organization was permitted to guarantee was 16,500 heads of families for the year.

Following the May Day disturbances of 1921 and the report of the Haycraft Commission that followed, the government issued a new ordinance, pronounced by the High Commissioner on 3 June, 1921, and introduced into the White Paper issued by the Colonial Secretary Winston Churchill in 1922. The new ordinance established the absorptive capacity principle as the guideline for the Mandatory immigration policy. Under this principle immigrants were divided into four categories: people with independent means sufficient for their absorption (Category A or Capitalists); people without means but with definite prospects for employment (Category C or Labour); people whose maintenance is guaranteed without joining the labor market, such as students and religious functionaries (Category B); and family members dependent on local residents (Category D or Dependents). Despite the fact that the Mandate granted the Jewish Agency with a statutory status regarding immigration (no. 4 of the Mandate draft) the sole authority over immigrants in categories A, B, and D lay in the hands of the government. The numbers of Labour certificates C were decided upon the government's estimations of absorption possibility, and most of them (but not all) were handed over to the JA for distribution.[18]

In April 1924, in order to prevent the entrance of low-middle class immigrants with meager financial means a new provision elevated the minimal requirement for a Capitalist certificate to 500 pounds and incorporated in a new immigration ordinance issued in September 1925.

The Immigration Ordinance of 1925 remained principally in effect until 1933. In 1927, though, following an economic crisis in Palestine, Category A was divided

---

16 Alroey (1993).
17 Mosek (1976).
18 *Report of the Zionist Executive to the 13th Zionist Congress, 1923*, 188–189; Halamish (2006), 19–23.

into a few sub-categories and the capital requirement for immigrants in category Ai (independent means) rose in practice to 1,000 pounds. This practice was incorporated in a regulation in April 1930.

The main concern guiding these regulations was the economic prospect of the immigrants to integrate successfully into the country's economy. However, economic consideration involved by definition some political concerns, regarding the growing conflict between Jews and Arabs. During the course of the 1930s, political concerns guided the government at an escalating pace. In the wake of the Arab revolt and the ensuing political unrest in 1936, the British government introduced the political criteria to limit immigration. In the summer of 1937 the government decided upon a maximum of 12,000 immigrants for the year, which meant not only the reduction of the schedules of Labour certificates, but also a drastic limitation on the entrance of Capitalists. The Colonial Secretary MacDonald's White Paper of May 1939 incorporated these regulations within a new long-term immigration policy aimed at imposing a halt to Jewish immigration and keeping the existing rate of Jewish population in Palestine at no more than one third. The new regulations put a limit of 75,000 Jewish immigrants over five years altogether before a complete halt.[19]

Up to 1937, within the given framework, the Jewish Agency had a limited option to control the distribution of certificates within the category of Labour. People who were eligible to immigrate as tourists, capitalists and returning residents had to apply to the British consul in their respective countries of residence. They would get the visa without any other intervention.

The procedures with the Labour category involved, from the summer of 1922 on, the Jewish Agency on two levels. In the first instance, the JA presented the government with estimation of the number of workers who could be absorbed in the country in the following half-year period, and after negotiation the government decided on the amount (Schedule) of Labour certificates for that period. In the second instance, the JA – through its Immigration Department – was responsible for the distribution of a certain number of the scheduled Labour certificates among some 25 Palestine Offices in the Diaspora. The government preserved its control in a few ways: The schedules were not defined merely in quantities, but also in qualities of age and skills. Following allocation by the Palestine Offices, the consuls were not formally bound to grant the visas in accordance with the given selection. Moreover, immigrants with visas were re-examined in the ports of Palestine and were sometimes rejected.[20] Since 1933, with the Nazi seizure of

---

19 Halamish (2006), 49–98.
20 Ibid., 189–190.

power and the persecution of German Jews, the government interfered in direct allocation of certificates (over the authority of the JA) to Germany.[21]

The Zionist Immigration Department distributed the allotted schedule of certificates among the Palestine Offices according to pressures of demand. Polish Jewry, the largest European Jewish population outside of the Soviet Union and under harsh economic and political pressures within the newly established national state of Poland presented the highest demand. Poland thus received the largest number of immigration certificates. Since the allocated number of certificates was always below the request for immigration, the allocation to individuals by the Palestine Offices was an exacting matter. Each Palestine Office was directed by a committee composed of representatives of the various Zionist political parties, according to the election results to the Zionist Congress every two years.

Since the demand exceeded the supply of certificates, the Zionist Immigration Department introduced additional criteria to those defined by the government, such as a minimum time of *hakhshara* (training) in a Zionist run farm, etc. Therefore, those who belonged to pioneer youth movements and went through the HeHalutz (Pioneer umbrella organization of Labor Zionist youth movements) training had priority, which was translated into advantage for members of the leftist labor movements.

The maneuvering of the JA regarding the allocation of immigration certificates was, however, halted completely in 1937, when the government imposed the new rigid rules that vested the control over immigration exclusively in its own hands. The only exception was the special allocation of children and youth certificates that enabled the JA to establish the project *Aliyat HaNo'ar* (Youth *Aliya*, or Youth Immigration) and to bring from Nazi Central Europe between the years 1934–1939 about 5,000 children under the age of 17 years.[22]

Jewish Immigration to Palestine

Palestine, with its emerging potential for political and economic development under the British Mandate, became a favorably considered destination for Jewish immigrants already by the beginning of the 1920s. These immigrants came mainly from Russia and Poland. The commonly accepted division of this period into two waves of immigration, the Third *Aliya* between 1919–1923, and the Fourth *Aliya* during 1924–1929, is based on generalizations of contemporary images or stigmas,

---

21 Ibid., 302.
22 Hacohen (2011), 374.

does not reflect the yearly fluctuation, nor does it allow any analysis of the immigrant profiles over the whole period. Actually, the "long" decade witnessed the first wave of massive Jewish immigration to Mandatory Palestine of 1920–1926 and the relative lull of 1927–1931, with some recovery in 1932, making for a total inflow of 126,349 individuals in 1919–1932, of whom 48,300 got there in 1924–1925 alone.[23]

The immigration flow revived in 1933 and intensified thereafter to constitute the second massive influx of 228,170 people during 1933–1939. The advantage of Palestine was particularly noticeable in the first half of the 1930s. Following the recovery from the economic downturn of 1926–1927 and from the aftermath of the violent outbursts of 1929, the country entered a phase of economic prosperity and relatively stable political atmosphere until the mid-1930s. It was precisely at that time that the U.S., Britain, and most other countries struggled with the Great Depression, attempting, among other means, to limit the entry of people into their severely hit economies, which in turn lost much of their attractiveness as potential destinations.

Thus, the weight of Palestine in Jewish international migration grew from an already unprecedented 16 percent in 1920–1931, to no less than 65 percent in 1932–1935 (see Table 1 above). Note that in the first twelve years (1920–1931) out of a total of 733,000 internationally migrating Jews, 115,000 immigrated to Palestine, with 360,000 moving to the U.S., whereas in the four years of 1932–1935, the number of Palestine's arrivals reached a record number of 161,000, representing 65 percent of the total Jewish migration.[24]

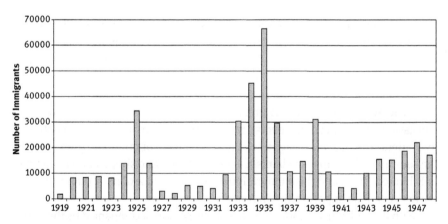

Graph 1: Jewish immigration to Palestine, 1919–1948
Source: Metzer (2008), 222

---

23 Metzer (2008).
24 See also Figure 1 hereafter.

In late 1935, economic fortune turned against Palestine; a depression followed soon by the Arab revolt of 1936–1939 badly affected the economic and political atmosphere and brought about the new immigration restrictions adding another factor to the downturn of Palestine as an immigration destination. In 1936–1939 only 86,000 immigrants reached Palestine, who constituted only 35 percent of total Jewish world migration. This number was only slightly larger than the number of Jewish immigrants to the U.S. in those years (80,700 people). Palestine's position as destination deteriorated further during the spring of 1939, with the White Paper of the government restricting to a minimum legal Jewish immigration. At that time, following the Nazi aggression (the *Anschluss* in Austria in March 1938, the *Kristallnacht* devastations of November 1938, and the occupation of Czechoslovakia in March 1939), the U.S. and Britain introduced new regulations easing somewhat the entry of refugees into their territories. With the beginning of recovery from the Great Depression the attractiveness of the Western countries as destinations grew as well. Consequently, the bulk of the Jewish refugee emigration from Central Europe reached, by the end of the 1930s and the beginning of the 1940s, the shores of Britain and the U.S., and not of Palestine, which was only reached by a tiny number of some 2,000 illegal immigrants.

British Immigration Policy

The basis for the British immigration policy was set up already in 1905. The Aliens Act of 1905 (in British law the term "alien" is used to designate someone who is not a citizen of Britain or the British Empire) was the first piece of immigration legislation in 20th century Britain. One of its main objectives was to control Jewish immigration from Eastern Europe that saw a significant increase after 1880. The Act introduced for the first time immigration controls and registration, and gave the Home Secretary overall responsibility for immigration and nationality matters. The Act was designed to prevent paupers or criminals from entering the country and set up a mechanism to deport those who slipped in. The Act had only limited effect, and the immigration declined because of perceptions of much greater economic opportunities in America.

With the outbreak of World War I the Aliens Act was accompanied by the Aliens Registration Act, which made mandatory the registration of all aliens over the age of 16 with the police and, for the first time in history, the government had some reasonably accurate information concerning migrants in terms of numbers, places of residence, occupations and race. Following the war, the 1905 Act was replaced by a much more stringent one, the Aliens Restriction (Amendment) Act 1919. The requirement for aliens to register with the police was renewed, and the act added further restrictions and consolidated powers of the Home Secretary to deport aliens already in U.K. The 1919 Aliens Restrictions Act and the ensuing Aliens Order of 1920 also added new restrictions to the civil and employment rights of aliens already resident in Britain. It virtually ended Jewish immigration to Britain until the 1930s. In addition, the earlier unconditional right of asylum was severely limited in 1926. From that year, aliens could enter the country only temporarily, unless they were granted a permit from the Ministry of Labour and had some visible means of support. This legislation, originally renewable annually, determined Britain's severely restrictive immigration policy during the Great Depression years. The government reacted to the early outrages of the Nazi regime by confirming that Britain was not a country of immigration, citing the country's already large population, high unemployment levels, and an ostensible fear of aggravating local anti-Semitism.[25]

The picture, however, changed substantially in 1938 following the *Anschluss* in Austria and the *Kristallnacht* pogrom. Unlike the U.S., Britain introduced in response a new refugee policy by issuing new categories of entry that enabled the mass entrance of refugees. These included: transmigration permits for holders of U.S. visas who had to wait to be included in future U.S. quotas; domestics hired by private families; holders of permits for vocational training in England (mainly in industry); Home Office special work permits, and "Blue Cards" for those over 60 years old whose support was guaranteed by private or other agencies.[26]

Jewish Immigration to Britain

In terms of interwar Jewish intercontinental migration Britain did not count for the larger part of the period. However, regarding Central European refugees after 1938 Britain filled an important role, becoming one of the three major destinations dealt with in this book.

The estimates regarding Jewish immigration to Britain vary in the 1930s. Official statistics did not distinguish between tourists and immigrants. In view of these constraints, the following estimates seem to be the most reliable. About 83,000 Jews from Central Europe appear to have arrived in Britain between 1933 and 1941. The great part of this movement took place after 1938.[27] Besides,

---

25 Shatzkes (2002), 47.

26 Refugee Aid Committee Report (April 1939), Wiener Library London (WLL), MF CBF, reel 2, file 190.

27 Rosenstock (1956); Salomon Adler-Rudel, "Die jüdischen Refugees in England" (1943), Salomon Adler-Rudel Collection, Leo Baeck Institute New York (LBIANY), AR 4473; Strickhausen (1998).

Britain became the destination for the project *Kindertransport* (Children Transfer) which encompassed some 10,000 children and youth from Germany, Austria and Czechoslovakia after the *Kristallnacht* pogrom up until the war.

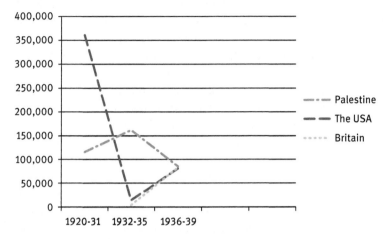

Graph 2: Jewish interwar migration: The proportion received by three countries

Table 2: Jewish interwar migration: Proportion received by three countries

Period	Total		Palestine		U.S.A.		Britain	
	thousands	%	thousands	%	thousands	%	thousands	%
1920–31	733	100	115	16	360	49		
1932–35	249	100	161	65	14	6	4	2
1936–39	246	100	86	35	81	31	83	34
1920–39	1,227	100	362	29	455	37	87	8

Sources: For Palestine and the U.S.A. see Table 1, above. For Britain: Rosenstock (1956); Salomon Adler-Rudel, "Die jüdischen Refugees in England" (1943), Salomon Adler-Rudel Collection, Leo Baeck Institute New York (LBIANY), AR 4473; Strickhausen (1998), 251–269.

In Conclusion

World War I had a huge, worldwide impact on the history of migration in general and of Jewish migrations, in particular. The prewar era was marked by mass Jewish overseas immigration from Eastern Europe, mainly the Russian Empire to Western Europe and the Americas. Within 40 years (1875–1914) about 2,200,000

Jews immigrated to overseas destinations, of whom about two thirds – 1,300,000 – went to the United States.

The postwar era was marked with dramatic geo-political and economic changes that caused major shifts in the source of world Jewish migration. Following the political changes in Eastern Europe, Russia ceased to be the main source and its place was taken by Poland and, following the Nazi seizure of power, Poland was joined by Germany and the rest of Central Europe. This migration became more and more a forced movement out, that encountered huge problems in finding destinations, namely a refugee movement.

The international arena changed dramatically in regards to immigration possibilities. Growing immigration restrictions were imposed by the countries that had served before the war as major destinations for immigration, particularly the U.S.A., besides Argentine and Canada. On the other hand, Palestine emerged as a major destination until the mid-1930s, and was replaced by Britain by the end of the 1930s. Moreover, while during the years 1901–1914 the U.S. took in the great majority of immigrants (1,346,000 out of 1,602,000, or 84 percent),[28] in the postwar era roles changed. Out of a total of 1,227, 000 Jewish immigrants between the years 1920–1939, the U.S. took in about 37 percent only. The major overseas destination beside the U.S. was Palestine, which took in 29 percent of the total. Among other countries, chief destinations were Argentina, with about 103,000 immigrants (8 percent of the total); Britain, which took in 83,000 immigrants (7 percent) during the late 1930s, and Canada, with about 53,000 immigrants (4 percent of the total) throughout the years 1920–1939.[29]

Moreover, since the U.S. was the major option anyhow, one should consider not only the proportion of immigrants it received, but its role in limiting migration options, namely in limiting radically the actual migration altogether. While the yearly overseas Jewish migration during the years 1901–1914 was estimated at an average of 115,000,[30] the yearly average of the 20 interwar years was cut by almost half, 61,000. In other words: after World War I, against the growing pressure to emigrate from Europe, Jewish overseas immigration was cut by half.

---

28 Lestschinsky (1965), 141–142.
29 Lestschinsky (1944), 8.
30 Lestschinsky (1965), 139.

Chapter 3
German Jewry in the Interwar Period and the Push Factors for Emigration

The Weimar Period

After World War I, Germany was in a state of upheaval. With its economic infra-structure badly damaged by the war, the infant republic faced a complete break-down of law and order. The country was flooded by demoralized former soldiers, communist and nationalist uprisings broke out, and the government was power-less to restrain them. National elections were held in January 1919, but the newly elected national assembly which convened in Weimar to draft a new republican constitution did not return to Berlin until September. The vacuum created by the non-assertive Social-Democratic government was filled by the *Freikorps* vigilante groups, and early in 1919 they brutally murdered the heads of the communist group Spartacus, Rosa Luxemburg and Karl Liebknecht, and later assassinated the Jewish Bavarian prime minister, Kurt Eisner, and his fellow government members, many of them Jews, among them Gustav Landauer. The bitter defeat and humiliating terms of the Treaty of Versailles sparked an aggressive national-ism that laid the blame for Germany's disgrace on the shoulders of the republic. Furthermore, the war debt and reparations led to runaway inflation which com-pletely spun out of control by 1922. As the monetary system broke down in 1923 the economy teetered on the verge of total collapse. Unemployment was rampant, millions lost their livelihood, and the crime rate rose dramatically. Acts of ter-rorism were carried out by a paramilitary underground, and the Jewish foreign minister, Walther Rathenau, was assassinated. In November 1923 the Nazi Party, established in 1919, attempted a *coup* in Munich (the Beer Hall *Putsch*). Only toward the end of 1923 and the beginning of 1924, when the Stresemann govern-ment managed to bring inflation under control, did German life slowly resume some semblance of normalcy for the first time since the war.

On the surface, 1924–1929 were peaceful years. However, the foundations of the republic were none too solid and governments based on shaky coalitions came and went. At the same time, the conservative and reactionary elements in German society were perpetuated through the administration, the courts, the military and the educational system. These tendencies were strengthened by the 1925 election of Paul von Hindenburg, a representative of monarchism and Prus-sian militarism to the presidency. The rebuilding of the economy was slow and

DOI 10.1515/9783110501650-004

plagued by setbacks. The Nazi Party, reorganized in 1925, launched a massive propaganda campaign and became increasingly influential.

Nonetheless, it seemed that the democratic system was becoming entrenched and the economy was on the road to recovery. Germany, and Berlin in particular, was gaining its former eminence as a center of European culture, and the arts, literature and science flourished. In the eyes of its citizens and others around the world, the Weimar Republic was a bastion of modern culture, and an intellectual trendsetter. The signing of the Locarno treaties and the evacuation of the Ruhr Valley in 1925, followed by the acceptance of Germany into the League of Nations in 1926, seemed to signify that old animosities had been laid aside.

German Jewry, which had prospered and attained a large measure of political and civic equality before the war, flourished even more under the Weimar Republic. All remaining discrimination was abolished and there were no restrictions on participation in German public life. Jews figured prominently in the leadership of the ruling Social-Democratic and Democratic parties and held senior positions in the civil service.

The Jews of the Weimar Republic suffered from the same economic hardships as other Germans, but their recovery was rapid. As the last professional restrictions of the monarchist period fell away, they established themselves in the universities, civil service, law, business, banking and the free professions. Certain spheres were virtually monopolized by the Jews, and their contribution to journalism, literature, theater, music, the plastic arts and entertainment was considerable. The Jews were prominent in intellectual circles and scientific research, and some scholars contend that they were ultimately the wellspring of "Weimar culture," the bustling creative activity that built Germany's reputation as a major cosmopolitan center.

So heady and enticing was German life that many Jews lunged ahead prepared to sacrifice their Jewishness for the sake of total integration. Intermarriage soared to 45 percent, and many Jews converted or severed their ties with the Jewish community.

Alongside civil rights fully enjoyed by the Jews as individuals, the Weimar Republic placed no limits on the development of Jewish communal and cultural life. Recognized on a democratic secular basis, Jewish communities were allowed to work freely in the spheres of religion, education, health and welfare, and developed a broad array of services and organizations. Nevertheless, anti-Semitism was far from dead throughout the 1920s. The *Centralverein Deutscher Staatsbürger jüdischen Glaubens* (The Central Association of German Citizens of the Jewish Faith, CV), the largest Jewish organization, channeled much of its energy into fighting anti-Semitism, but underneath was the belief that the forces of progress, which had never been stronger, would eventually win. Most of the Jews of the

Weimar Republic, both those who were totally assimilated and those who kept up their Jewish affiliation, were united in the belief that full political, social and cultural integration in the German homeland was only a matter of time.[1]

The Demographic Profile of German Jewry

According to the German census of 1925, the number of Jews in Germany was about 564,000. This number declined steadily thereafter. The decrease was strongly combined with process of aging following urbanization and growing birth control. In 1933 over 31 percent were more than forty years old, due mainly to the high death rate within this relatively aged Jewish community, but which remained above its declining birthrate. The tendency for intermarriage, that continued to accelerate, was another cause for the Jewish community to shrink, since most of the children of intermarried couples were not raised as Jews.[2] By 1933, the Jewish population in Germany counted about 500,000,[3] which reflects a decline of 65,000 persons, or 12 percent within eight years.

The occupational and age structure of Weimar Jews as of 1933 is reflected in Table 3. Only 248,000 individuals, less than half of the Jewish population of the early 1930s, were gainfully occupied. About 20 percent lived on rents and pensions or welfare. Most of the others were dependents. Of the active breadwinners, most were in commerce and only a minority in professions. Moreover, despite the pace of economic mobility and urbanization – by 1933 more than half of the German Jews lived in the ten big cities (in Berlin alone 160,000) – only a small proportion was able to climb the occupational ladder and reach its highest echelons, whereas most were small merchants or wage earners.[4]

An additional factor in the demographic decline was the unstable economy of post-World War I Weimar Republic, which pushed more than 600,000 Germans, plus some 60,000 Jews, to emigrate.[5]

However, despite the dominance of economic push factors, anti-Semitism seems to have played a role in driving young people to decide on emigration even before the Nazi seizure of power, particularly from 1930 on, with the growing strength of the Nazi Party.

---

1 Lavsky (1996), 39–42.
2 Barkai (1997), 37–49.
3 See different estimations in Chapter 4.
4 Barkai (1997); Traub (1936).
5 See Chapter 4 hereafter.

Table 3: The demographic profile of German Jewry, June 1933

Age*		Occupation**	
Age Groups	%		%
0–15	16.5	Commerce and Communication	61.3
16–24	11.7	Industry and Handicrafts	23.1
25–39	23.9	Public Service and Professions	12.5
40–59	31.5	Agriculture and Forests	1.7
60 and over	16.3	Household Services	1.4
Total	100.0	Total	100.0

* Calculated on the basis of table 3a in Strauss (1980), 318.
** Barkai (1997), 40; Traub (1936), 10–11, 14–17.

The Nazi Era

The Nazi seizure of power on 30 January, 1933 caused a significant upheaval of Jewish emigration. This time, counter to the emigration during the Weimar era which was mainly a Jewish and non-Jewish response to economic factors, in the Nazi era the main factor was the Nazi persecution of Jews, though at first it was combined with persecution of various groups beside Jews, such as the communists and the cultural-intellectual elite, which included many Jews, beside non-Jews, and thus might have obscured the unique Jewish issue. Moreover, the changing pace and intensity of Nazi measures against Jews fluctuated in the first years of the Nazi regime and the gap between decrees and their implementation changed from time to time and from place to place.

The Dynamics of Nazi Anti-Jewish Measures

By the beginning of the 1930s, following the Nazi achievement in the September 1930 elections, harassment against Jews occurred more often than before, openly and systematically. Street terror intensified dramatically with the Nazi seizure of power on 30 January, 1933, when Adolf Hitler was summoned by the President, General von Hindenburg, to establish the government, and he became the

Note: This section is based primarily on Barkai (1989); Barkai and Mendes-Flohr (1997), 193–368; Friedländer (1997); Matthäus and Roseman (2010).

Kanzler (Chancellor, Prime Minister). Official pressure to expel Jews from public institutions and from the economy began immediately and gathered strength after the Nazi election victory on 5 March, 1933. However, the steps against the Jews, aimed to create a pure "Aryan" public sphere and "healthy" culture, were very much involved with steps against opponents or potential opponents to the Nazi regime, as well as to eradicate all kinds of "pervasive" or "degenerate" cultures. Therefore, the initial targets of Nazi persecution were Jews and non-Jews alike, as manifested by the burning of the books on 10 May, 1933. The cultural domain was the first from which Jews (and "leftists") were massively expelled, and since the people concerned were well known scientists, artists and intellectuals, they were people of the world and could respond relatively easily by immigrating to welcoming foreign countries.

Not less than the "degenerate culture," primary political targets were the communists. After the Reichstag fire of 27 February, 1933, almost ten thousand communists were arrested and imprisoned in newly created concentration camps. Dachau was inaugurated on 1 April. Although the *Nationalsozialistische Deutsche Arbeiterpartei* (National Socialist German Workers Party, NSDAP) failed to gain an absolute majority in the 5 March Reichstag elections, they managed to create an atmosphere of emergency which led the Reichstag to place in their hands absolute political power, and to abolish all remnants of potential risk, such as trade unions and political parties other than the NSDAP.

Indeed, attacks against Jews became a matter of daily life, but they remained local events carried out by Storm Troopers (SA) and their followers. This violence intensified following the March elections, but the first orchestrated anti-Jewish public terror act was the one-day boycott of 1 April, 1933 of Jewish-owned businesses. Even then, though, the Jewish policy of Hitler didn't seem to be consistent. Pressure on private enterprises was not homogenous. During the first years of the regime there were indications of moderation on the part of big businesses dealing with non-Aryan firms. Pressure to take over aimed mainly at smaller, mid-sized enterprises, at least until the fall of 1937. This temporary moderation was motivated by the Nazi recognition of both the importance of the Jews in the economic recovery process, and by their considering the possibility of foreign economic retaliation, Jewish and non-Jewish.

Another feature typifying the Nazi policy in Jewish matters was its primary fixation on Eastern European immigrants. However, the first anti-Jewish law – of 7 April, 1933 – was the Civil Service Law that prohibited the employment of any non-Aryan or a descendent of a non-Aryan parent or grandparent. This prohibition was applied among others to 1,200 university professors, and thousands of school teachers, chemists, engineers, doctors, dentists and lawyers. For example, out of about 5,000 Jewish lawyers, almost 2,000 who worked in the public services were fired.[6] Another law, excluding Jewish lawyers from the bar, was confirmed on 11 April. These laws affected only a relatively small number of Jewish civil servants and lawyers, since under pressure from Hindenburg, war veterans and veteran civil servants were exempted. Nevertheless, these laws were decreed under public pressure and in the context of spreading violence against Jews, and were supported by civil organizations such as the National Association of Lawyers. Next in line were the Jewish physicians. Those employed in clinics and hospitals run by the national health insurance were already expelled from their position by 22 April. However, Hitler refrained from doing anything drastic against Jewish physicians as such since nearly 11 percent of all practicing German physicians were Jews. Jewish engineers were also thrown out of the civil service, but their case was a little different due to their relatively low proportion in general, and in the civil service in particular. Moreover, the guilds of engineers and technical professions were much less interested in politics and more indifferent to continuation of Jewish membership[7]

The next step was the 25 April Law against the Overcrowding of German Schools and Universities, which was aimed against non-Aryans students. But after these few measures taken in 1933, anti-Jewish politics subsided and fluctuated. On the one hand, in many places the entrance to bathing and entertainment facilities was denied for Jews, but on the other hand there were not clear guidelines and some of the high-ranking Nazi officials continued to entertain themselves in Jewish-owned facilities. From early 1935 on, popular violence against Jews intensified with the call against the *"Rassenschande"* (Race Defilement) which led to the issuance of the Nuremberg Laws, downgrading the Jews from the status of legal citizens to legal subjects, and denied them the right to marry or have sexual relations with non-Jews. These laws, however, did not aim to erase Jewish life from Germany but to create a full separation between the Germans as the *"Volksgemeinschaft"* (the People's Community) and the Jews, and could therefore be perceived as measures facilitating and ordering the continuance of Jewish existence in Germany. Indeed, from then on, and during the year 1936, the year of the Olympic Games in Berlin, the atmosphere cleared and hopes that the Jewish problem had been solved on a racial basis without violence were planted.

Before long, however, the Nazi regime started to take economic steps against the Jews, confiscating Jewish businesses and properties, denying Jewish students from submitting their doctoral dissertations (from 1937 on), and so on. The road to eradicating Jewish existence in Germany was now cleared. The Jewish population

---

6 Niederland (1996), 71–72.
7 Mock (1986).

declined from about half a million at the beginning of 1933 to 360–365,000 by the beginning of 1938. The proportion of Berlin Jewry grew from about 32 percent (160,000) in 1933 to about 38 percent (140,000) of the declining Jewish population due to accelerating internal immigration from small impoverished places. About 60–70 percent of Jewish businesses existing in 1933 had already been confiscated or *Aryanized* by the beginning of 1938, most of them retail businesses. Throughout 1938 economic persecution continued vigorously. By December 1938 only 6,000 Jewish firms and 3,750 Jewish retail businesses still existed. The economic destruction was accompanied by a process of implementation of racial laws emanating from the Nuremberg Citizenship Law. Jewish religious associations and regional community associations lost their legal status. Doctors and lawyers lost their licenses and special taxes were levied on individual Jews and Jewish communities. In July 1938 Jewish passports had to carry stamp of the letter *J*, and in August their holders had to add Jewish names – Israel and Sarah.

The year 1938 was defined by Jewish leaders as the final stage in the liquidation of German Jewry, which reached its climax in the *Reichskristallnacht*[8] Pogrom of 9–10 November, 1938. Hundreds of synagogues were burned down and thousands of shops and residences ruined and robbed by German mobs, in what was an orchestrated pogrom all over the Reich. Some 30,000 Jewish men were deported to concentration camps (about 10 percent of the remaining Jewish population, which means that every family was hit by deportation of at least one member).[9] The prisoners were tortured and many died there, and others were released on the condition that they emigrate by the end of the year. The pogrom was a turning point. From now on the Nazi authorities focused on forced emigration, and for that purpose isolated the Jews, deprived them of all their properties, closed all Jewish institutions and publishing houses, and established the *Centralstelle für Jüdische Auswanderung* (Center for Jewish Emigration).[10]

The year 1941 marked a new turning point in the intensive process of deprivation and ghettoization that followed the outbreak of the war in September 1939. Against the background of the Nazi invasion to the Balkans and the Soviet Union, along with the breaking diplomatic relations by the U.S.A., in September 1941 Jews were forced to wear the Yellow Star, and in October emigration was forbidden altogether.

Nazi persecution measures fluctuated over the years, and included many steps that contradicted their wish to encourage Jewish emigration, such as confiscating properties and denying civil documents. "The absolute figures and

---

8 The term – a euphemism – was invented to reflect the spectacle of broken glass and was used by the Nazis to actually hide the murderous character of the pogrom.
9 Zimmermann (2013), 28.
10 Zariz (1990).

percentages of the needy increased from year to year, but [by 1937] not all German Jews were destitute as yet. Many still had property and assets; these could serve as a source for financing emigration but were also key factors in inducing them to stay on. This is particularly true of the broad middle classes."[11] Already by the beginning of 1930s the Brüning government introduced the Reich Flight Tax to prevent the flight of capital abroad. The Nazis transformed it into a legal measure to plunder Jewish property. Until 1938 it functioned as a factor in the decisions of affluent Jews about whether to emigrate. After May 1934 it was levied on all assets of RM 50,000 or more, based on the last estimated value of the property. The process of *Aryanization* resulted in selling property below real value and thus significantly increased the rate of the tax. Moreover, a potential emigrant could not transfer his money abroad but had to leave it deposited in a special blocked account in Reichsmarks. The sale of Reichsmarks from this account for foreign currency entailed a considerable loss due the set exchange rate. The *Reichsbank* constantly reduced its payments to the depositor, and by September 1939 these payments reached the record of four percent of the original value. In practice, emigrating German Jews were actually able to take along only a small fraction of their capital.[12] On the other hand, responding to Nazi persecution by emigration was very much dependent on possibilities. This argument means that the push factors as well as the pull factors were not decisive in pointing to emigration as the best option in response to the new situation.

The German-Jewish Public Response to Nazism: Emigration?

German Jews presumably should have reacted to Nazi persecution with mass emigration. Indeed, it can be argued that German Jews were so immersed in German culture and believed so deeply that Nazism was only a tragic accident that they neglected or postponed any decision to get organized for emigration. While this argument might be partly true in explaining individual responses, it is dubious in relation to responses of the community and organizations' leadership for three reasons. First, possibilities for Jewish emigration were very limited; second, emigration was not the only way to respond to changing circumstances; and third, Nazi persecution was not thought to be leading eventually to total annihilation. Until 1938 German Jews calculated their options between going and staying as potential emigrants, who are still able to rationally evaluate the pros and cons,

---

11 Barkai (1989), 99.
12 Ibid., 99–100.

timing and destination for their move, not as refugees who had no choice. Beyond that, they regarded the prospects of time left to get organized for even a transitional existence in Germany as much longer than it turned out to be in reality.

Starting in 1933 and until the outbreak of the war, some 270,000 Jews out of 517,000 did emigrate. Until 1935, only 90,000 did so, while the vast majority left Germany only following the *Kristallnacht* pogrom of November 1938. Moreover, most of the early emigrants moved to neighboring countries, assuming that their move would be for a transitional period. Of those who made the decision to emigrate for good, a significant portion made their way to Palestine, which became between 1933 and 1935 the preferred single overseas destination. The fact that Palestine took the lead during the early period is explained by its advantages over other options. Palestine under the British Mandate enjoyed prosperity and consequently exercised a flexible immigration policy contrary to other countries, mainly the U.S.A. that suffered from economic depression and introduced very harsh and rigid immigration policies.[13]

The following sections deal with the response to Nazism by emigration from two perspectives: the public and the individual.

German Jews were not organized under any inclusive organization. The main pragmatic response of the majority, represented in the *Centralverein* and in the large Jewish communities, to the rise of Nazism was the establishment of the *Zentralausschuss der deutschen Juden für Hilfe und Aufbau* (Central Committee of German Jews for Welfare and Rehabilitation, hereafter – the Welfare Committee) and the *Zentrallstelle für jüdische Wirtschaftshilfe* (Central Bureau for Economic Assistance), in April 1933, in order to enable the continuity of Jewish life in and against the backdrop of the new circumstances.[14] These institutions were the initiative of all the pre-existing Jewish organizations, Zionists and non-Zionists, and were in fact the first united Jewish institutions in German-Jewish history. The establishment of an all-inclusive representative organization, the *Reichsvertretung der deutschen Juden* (National Representation of German Jews, RV), followed suit in September 1933 and sent a representative to the Welfare Committee. The RV published its raison d'etre recognizing the fact that the existence and the future of German Jews were dependent and conditioned on their unity. It did not even raise the possibility of giving up or neglecting the continuation of Jewish life in Germany, but aimed to construct new foundations for that purpose by negotiating with the new regime and by conducting, together with the two forerunner

---

13 See Chapter 2.
14 The following discussion is mainly based on Margaliot and Cochavi (1998), vol. 1, 121–210.

committees – which merged with the RV in December 1934 – a large scale vocational retraining, economic and welfare activity.

At this stage, the Jewish leadership tried to stop emigration, arguing that emigration is not a real solution and endangers the possibility to construct a new Jewish existence in Germany. The main assumption was that if emigration was to be an option, it should be carefully prepared for the future and would not apply for the majority of German Jews.

The one Jewish organization that had long before propagated, prepared and organized emigration was the *Zionistische Vereinigung für Deutschland* (the Zionist Federation of Germany – ZVfD). The Palestine Office – an extension of the Jewish Agency (JA) Immigration Department in Berlin – was responsible for training, preparing and organizing potential immigrants within the framework of the Palestine Government immigration policy. Facing the Nazi threat, the Zionist movement in Germany was viewed by many German Jews as a safe means of access for immigration to the one country that was relatively open for immigration, and they joined the Zionist ranks in order to have this access sooner or later. A total of 10,000 Jews paid membership dues in 1932 compared with 22,500 at the end of 1935, not counting 7,000 members who had already emigrated during this period. From the standpoint of *Shekel* purchases (the right to vote in the elections to the World Zionist Congress which convened every two years) the increase was even more striking. On the eve of the 17th Zionist Congress in Basel, 1931, the number of *Shekel* buyers in Germany was 7,500; by the 19th Congress in Lucerne in 1935, the figure had soared to 57,200. By the same token, membership in the HeHalutz (The Pioneer) movement, which ran the Zionist agricultural training farms for youngsters, rose from 5,000 in April 1933 to 16,000 by late 1935, most of them "new" Zionists. Thousands of young people flocked to the various Zionist youth movements, elevating their total membership to more than 40,000 by early 1936. The number of subscribers to the Zionist bi-weekly *Jüdische Rundschau* rose from 4,000 to 30,000 after 1 April, 1933, and reached 40,000 in 1935. Similar dramatic increase occurred in the number of donors to the Zionist financial institutions, the Jewish National Fund (JNF), and the Jewish Foundation Fund (*Keren Hayesod*, KH). During the spring and summer of 1933, the information bureau of the Palestine Office in Berlin was swamped by 600–800 calls a day.[15]

In response to the unprecedented huge demand for immigration as opposed to the limited supply of certificates (visas to Palestine) German Zionists together with the JA and the World Zionist Organization (WZO) fostered the increase of settlement possibilities and the economic absorptive capacity of Palestine, which

---

15 Lavsky (1996), 235–238.

would allow an increase in the allocation of immigration certificates by the Palestine Government. In 1933 a triple-branch organization was launched: The old Berlin Palestine Office; the new London based Central Bureau for the Settlement of German Jews in Palestine headed by Chaim Weizmann, the President of the World Zionist Organization; and the German Department of the JA in Jerusalem headed by Arthur Ruppin, the long-standing director of Jewish settlement in Palestine. At the same time, they played on the same ground with the Nazi regime that was both keen on limiting the transfer of hard currency and interested in Jewish emigration, and reached the Transfer Agreement, which was ratified by the Economy Minister in August 1933. There was also a higher exchange rate for the *Reichsmark* than the usual one for emigrants, which in this case also had to be deposited in a special blocked account. This agreement made it easier for immigrants to Palestine to acquire a Capitalist visa which required a minimum of 1,000 Pounds. By 1939 about 140 million *Reichsmarks* (approximately £8 million) had been transferred to Palestine on the basis of this agreement.[16]

Besides its activity on behalf of *aliya* (immigration to Palestine), German Zionists followed the calls of Robert Weltsch, the chief editor of the *Jüdische Rundschau* "*Ja-sagen zum Judentum*" (say Yes to Judaism) and "*tragt ihn mit Stolz den gelben Fleck*" (wear the Yellow Star proudly)[17] to expand and deepen Jewish spiritual self-respect in Germany. These two activities complemented one another, as there was no chance for immediate mass emigration, even to Palestine. Organizing Jewish life in Germany meant cooperation between Zionists and non-Zionists.

Following an ever growing frustration, which culminated in confronting the Nuremberg Laws of September 1935, the RV radically changed its agenda and put emigration and the Zionist cause on top, defining its most pressing targets in this order: 1. Jewish education, aimed at constructing self-respect in Jewish identity and vocational training with the prospect of emigration, mainly to Palestine, including Hebrew studies. 2. Programming Jewish emigration, in the first place to Palestine, including training, foreign connections, information, and economic arrangements and facilitating measures. 3. Welfare. 4. Economic existence. 5. Building the national home in Palestine.[18] From now on the main activity on behalf of emigration was carried out by three offices: The *Hauptstelle für jüdische Wanderfürsorge* (The Central Office for the Care of Jewish Migrants) assisted Eastern European Jews to return to their home countries and internal migrants;

---

16 Lavsky (1996), 246–247.
17 Titles of leading articles in the *Jüdische Rundschau* also printed in *Ja-Sagen zum Judentum: Eine Aufsatzreihe der "Jüdischen Rundschau" zur Lage der deutschen Juden* (Berlin: Verlag der "Jüdischen Rundschau," 1933).
18 Margaliot and Cochavi (1998), vol. 1, 141–143.

the Palestine Office of the JA was in charge of the immigration to Palestine; and the veteran association *Hilfsverein der Deutschen Juden* (Central Welfare Bureau of German Jews) assisted immigration to countries other than Palestine. Besides, many training farms were established in Germany and the neighboring countries for agricultural and vocational training, mostly run by the Zionist movement but also financed by other World Jewish funds and run by the ORT organization.

Figure 1: The last visit of Arthur Ruppin (2nd right), Head of the Jewish Agency's Central Bureau for the Settlement of German Jews, in Germany, with Rabbi Leo Baeck (1st left), Chair of the *Reichsvertretung der Juden in Deutschland*, 1938. Courtesy of the Central Zionist Archives.

Thus, the united body of German Jews, in which the largest Jewish organization – the *Centralverein* – had been in the past anti-Zionist, adopted the Zionist agenda due to the fact that the Zionist path had become a practical option for a large section of German Jews.

It seems that given the limitations mentioned, German Zionism was much more prepared to embark on emigration due to four qualities. First, psychological preparation; second, spiritual framework for Jewish identification; third, the ability to suggest a path out of Germany; and fourth, by understanding that emigration, sooner or later, was inevitable. On the other hand, the ZVfD, with its long-standing *Palestine-Centrism* and avoidance of any involvement with intra-German-Jewish communal activity, resulted in its being much less prepared for internal Jewish activity that was a necessity in the given situation. Against the background of very limited immigration possibilities Jewish leaders had to prepare for a long-term activity to sustain the Jewish community in Germany, even if the goal in the long run was emigration. The Zionist leaders were much less equipped with organizational and financial tools for that matter. Hence – in order to pursue both goals in parallel – continued Jewish life in Germany and preparation for immigration, particularly to Palestine – all Jewish organizations had to cooperate with one another. In practice, one goal did not rule out the other. The Zionist Organization provided the ideological organizational synthesis by promoting Jewish education and culture, pioneer training, vocational training and eventually emigration, preferably to Palestine. The CV and the communities provided their long-term experience and devotion to maintaining social and cultural activity aimed at the shrinking Jewish population whose situation was deteriorating.

Chapter 4
German-Jewish Emigration: Dimensions, Timing, Destinations

The Weimar Era

During the Weimar years, Jewish emigration was an integral part of the general emigration caused mainly by economic factors. Among about 600,000 emigrants in general, the estimated number of Jews was some 60,000, representing about 10 percent of the Jewish population according to the census of 1925.[1] The peak years of the general emigration were 1923, coinciding with the galloping inflation, with 115,000 emigrants, and 1925–1926, coinciding with the stabilization crisis, with 63,000 and 65,000 emigrants respectively.[2] Jewish emigration included great numbers of "alien" Eastern European Jews (who immigrated to Germany before or during World War I), especially during the years 1922–1925. Data regarding Jewish immigration to the U.S.A. and to Palestine indicate that the years 1923 and 1925–1926 were also the peak years of Jewish emigration. The galloping inflation of the years 1922–1923 hit mainly those dependent on salaries and rent. The deflation of 1925–1926, on the other hand, affected mainly small businesses where Jews in general were significantly present.[3]

As for the pull factors – the early to mid-1920s prosperity in Palestine coincided in time with the transition from inflation to deflation in Germany, making Palestine appealing for Jews who were mainly affected by the German inflation. Since many Zionists belonged to this group, it is quite difficult to separate the ideological from the material motivation for emigration. It seems, however, that the potential emigrants with Zionist inclination tended to combine the decision to acquire new skills with their Zionist ideology. Thus, they tended to prepare themselves for agricultural settlement or for other occupations that were considered useful for the intensified Zionist build-up in Palestine during 1924–1925 – the hay years of the Fourth *Aliya* (immigration wave to Palestine according to Zionist terminology).

---

1 Niederland (1996), 21–23: estimation of the negative balance of migration for the years 1925–1933, including Eastern European Jews leaving Germany is cited there as 35,000–40,000. However, this estimation does not relate to the years 1919–1925; therefore it is necessary to add an estimation of a minimum 25,000 Jewish emigrants for the missing six years.

2 Estimation of German emigrants, not including Jews, is based on Bickelman (1980), Table 1, p. 143 (overseas emigration); Niederland (1996), 28–29, citing yearly data for the years 1919–1932 in Petzina et al. (1978), 35.

3 See Table 3, above.

DOI 10.1515/9783110501650-005

Table 4: Number of Jewish immigrants from Germany to Palestine and the U.S.A.,1920–1932

Years	to Palestine	to the U.S.A.
1920		458
1921	360	838
1922	44	600
1923	149	864
1924	470	1,986
1925	963	521
1926	325	652
1927	84	546
1928	87	361
1929	302	235
1930	138	167
1931	122	98
1932	353	45
1920–32	3,306	7,371

Source: Niederland (1996), 26–27.

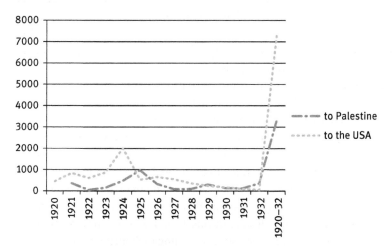

Graph 3: Number of Jewish immigrants from Germany to Palestine and the U.S.A., 1920–1932

Many Zionists came individually. For example, Ernst Simon went through intensive sports training and medical studies in order to become a gymnastics teacher
in Palestine, and was thus invited by Arthur Biram, the Reali High School head-
master in Haifa in 1924.[4] When Meta Flanter decided as a teenager to become a

---

4 Interview with Simon, OHD 10 (183).

Zionist and to immigrate to Palestine she first went through agricultural training and studied Hebrew. Only then did she immigrate, in late 1922.[5]

Figure 2: Jewish agricultural training farm near Berlin, 1928. Courtesy of the Central Zionist Archives.

But there were those who were particularly aware of anti-Semitic trends around them towards the end of the 1920s. This was the case of the young couple, Leo Wissmann and Judith Wechsler-Wissmann from Nuremberg, a city that was under the Nazi sway well before 1933. Both became Zionists, Leo studied carpentry and was invited by a carpenter in Jerusalem, and they got married and emigrated in 1931.[6] Eventually they opened their own very prestigious carpentry business.

Zionism was a driving factor, sometimes the dominant factor. This was the case with four siblings – out of the seven children of the physician Dr. Bernard Cohn – Charlotte, Helene and Rosa, who immigrated to Palestine in 1921, and

---

5 Interview with Flanter, OHD 7 (183).
6 Testimony by Judith Wissmann, in Zinke (2003), 134–240.

their brother Max who joined them with his family in 1923. All of them were educated by their father as Zionists and grew up as members in the Zionist youth movement. Charlotte (born 1893) studied architecture and was invited by Richard Kaufmann, chief architect in the Palestine Land Development Company, affiliated with the Jewish National Fund and in charge of designing new Jewish settlements, to join his team.[7]

On the other hand as reflected in the Table and Graph above, the U.S. continued to be a destination even after 1925 but ceased to play this role by the end of the decade, due to the economic crisis that broke out on Wall Street in 1929. The roles of both destination countries would however reverse dramatically during the first half of the 1930s.

The Nazi Era

Starting in 1933 and until the outbreak of the war, some 245,000 out of an estimated 512,000 at the beginning of 1933 did emigrate, namely 48 percent of the German-Jewish population. During the first three years of the Nazi regime, 1932–1935, only 90,000 did so, while the vast majority left Germany only following the *Kristallnacht* pogrom of November 1938.

The stages of Jewish emigration have been discussed at length in various studies, but references to the size of the Jewish population in 1933 vary. Barkai mentions once the number of 499,700, and in another context – the number of 502,799, while Traub refers to 517,000 and Strauss' estimation is 525,000 by religion but up to 867,000 Jewish and "non-Aryan" Germans were affected by the Nazi decrees.[8] These differences may be attributed to the scholar's choice of the exact time in 1933, since the process of emigration, which became the main cause of the demographic changes, accelerated dramatically from the end of 1932 and during the year 1933.

Strauss distinguishes between peak periods of Nazi persecution. The first, from 30 January, 1933, to mid-1933, the second during the summer of 1933, the third in 1935, divided between April and September, the fourth during 1936, the fifth in autumn 1937 and 1938, and the sixth in 1938–1941. Generally speaking, in the first upheaval of emigration from Nazi Germany in 1933, the majority of the emigrants went to neighboring Western and Eastern European countries,

---

7 Sonder (2006, 2009).
8 Barkai (1997), 38, 226, respectively; Strauss (1980), 313–361, Table 7, 326; Traub (1936). Strauss refers separately to the rate of non-German Jews emigrating from Germany, 328–329.

assuming that their move was only for a transition period. During the four years 1934–1937 emigration continued on the average of 23,000 emigrants yearly, and caused a further aging of the German-Jewish population, of which 45 percent were now older than 45 years.[9] The year 1938 marked a turning point: 39,000 Jews left Germany over the entire year,[10] with the exodus intensifying after the *Kristallnacht* pogrom of November 1938. About half of the total emigration from Nazi Germany, 100,000–150,000, left after mid-November 1938.[11] In May 1939, the Nazi census counted 213,390 "Jews by Religion" out of 318,350 Jews according to Nazi definition, including "Jews by Race" or "*Mischlinge*" – offspring of mixed marriages.

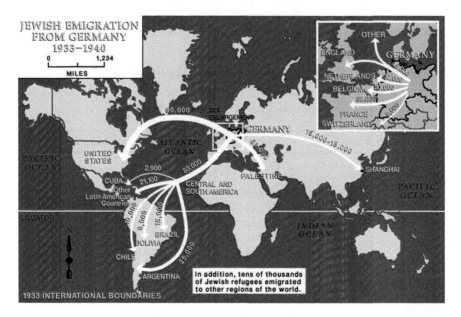

Figure 3: Map – emigration from Germany 1933–1940. Courtesy of the U. S. Holocaust Memorial Museum.

The fluctuations in the rate of emigration from 1933 until the war are presented in Graph 4 hereafter:

---

9 Council for German Jewry, First Annual Report for 1936, WLL.

10 Aid to Jews Overseas: Report of the Activities of American Jewish Joint Distribution Committee for the Year 1938 (hereafter: Joint Report), YIVO.

11 Zucker (2001).

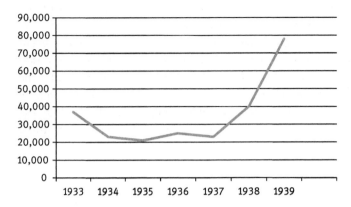

Graph 4: The dynamics of German-Jewish emigration, 1933–1939

The total number of emigrants is summarized in Table 5 below:

Table 5: German-Jewish emigration and population shrinkage, 1933–1945 (in thousands)

Year	Population	Emigration	Excess deaths	Deportations
1933	525.0	37.0 (38.0)*	5.5	
1934		23.0	5.5	
1935		21.0 (20.0)*	5.5	
1936		25.0	6.0	
1933–36		**106.0**		
1937		23.0	7.0	
1938		40.0	8.0	
May 1939	213.4			
1939		78.0**	10.0	
1938–39		**118.0**		
1933–39		**247.0**	**47.5**	
1940		15.0	8.0	10.0
May 1941	**169.0**			
Oct. 1941	164.0	8.0	4.0	25.0
1933–1941		**270.0**		
1942	139.0		7.5	73.0
1943	51.0	8.5	5.0	25.0
1944	14.5			1.0
1945	20.0–25.0			
Total		**278.0**	**72.0**	**134.0**

Source: Strauss (1980), 313–361, Table 7, 326.
* Slightly different yearly estimations and causes summarized by Benz (1998).
** Zariz (1990), 26, mentions the number 68,000, based on Blau (1950).

Some 247,000 Jews, almost a half of the German-Jewish population of 1933, left Germany before the war. But Jews continued to escape Germany afterwards. Between September 1939 – the outbreak of the war – and October 1941, when emigration was prohibited, about 25,500 more left Germany, and a few thousands more are estimated as managing to escape even thereafter.[12]

The yearly numbers of emigrants, however, do not mirror the sub-periods mentioned above but point to two upheavals of migration: 1933 and 1938/1939.

As can be learned from Table 5, emigration became the major factor in accelerating the ongoing population shrinkage. Since old people were naturally the last – if at all – people who were able to emigrate, shrinkage was accompanied by the rapid aging of the remaining Jewish population: The rate of those over 65 years old climbed from 10.5 percent in 1933 to 21.3 percent in the census of May 1939, and the proportion of children up to the age of 14 years went down from 15.9 percent to 7.5 percent, respectively. The gender composition also changed. While in 1933 women comprised 52.2 percent, in 1939 their proportion climbed to 57.5 percent. These proportions changed further dramatically during the following months of mass emigration until the outbreak of the war.[13]

Timing and Destination Choice

In the following discussion an attempt is made to evaluate the balance of push and pull factors on emigration decisions as illustrated by immigrants to the three destinations discussed in this book. Some questions are discussed relating to the dynamics and patterns of the emigration process, its rate and choice of destinations, and the connections between these and the varying social profiles of the emigrants in a comparative framework. This study adopts the distinction suggested by Niederland between what was still a "voluntary" emigration, albeit one motivated by harsh, even if indirect, pressure with constraints imposed by limited options during the first five years of the Nazi regime, and what amounted to brutal expulsions from late 1938 to early 1941.[14]

Table 6 illustrates the combination between timing and destination in general, and demonstrates the impact of the pull factors – the possibilities of these destinations as discussed in Chapter 2.

---

12 Zariz (1990), 43–45.

13 Barkai (1997), 226, based on the estimation of total 502,799 Jews by religion in 1933, and 213,930 Jews in May 1939.

14 Niederland (1996).

Table 6: German-Jewish immigration overseas: to Palestine, the U.S., and Britain 1933–1941, selected periods*

Period	From Germany		To Palestine		To the U.S.A.		To the U.K.	
	Number	%	Number	%	Number	%	Number	%
1933–1935	93,000	100.0	31,000	33.3	9,500	10.2	4,000	4.3
1933–1938	169,000	100.0	43,200	25.6	27,000	16.0	10,000	5.9
1938–1941	141,000	100.0	14,800	10.5	55,000	39.0	35,000	24.8
1933–1941	270,000	100.0	53,200	19.7	82,000	30.4	45,000	16.7

* Data on emigration from Germany based on Table 5, above; Data for immigration: Traub (1936); Joint Reports, 1936, 1937, 1938, YIVO; Barkai (1997), 227; Gelber (1990), 57.

Figure 4: People in the waiting room of the Palestine Office in Berlin, 1935. Courtesy of the Central Zionist Archives.

During the first phase of 1933–1935, Palestine was first among these three overseas destinations, but the picture changed dramatically in 1938, when Palestine lost its position as a welcoming destination. Of those who made an early decision to emigrate for good, a significant portion made their way to Palestine, which became between 1933 and 1935 the largest single overseas destination. The fact that Palestine took the lead during the early period is explained by its advantages over other options; Palestine under the British Mandate enjoyed prosperity and in consequence exercised a flexible immigration policy compared to other countries, mainly the U.S.A., that suffered from economic depression and introduced very harsh and rigid immigration policies.[15]

Figure 5: Zionist agricultural training farm, 1935. Courtesy of the Central Zionist Archives.

It is common knowledge that the year 1938, in particular after the *Kristallnacht* pogrom, was a turning point in the fate of German Jewry. Although Nazi persecution was a continuum that accelerated dramatically in 1937 and 1938, the events of November 1938 were crucial. It seems that any doubts regarding the possibility of staying in Germany were abruptly smashed. Indeed, from the point of view of the numbers of German-Jewish emigrants, this was the turning point.

But behind the numbers, the picture was much more complicated. Is it really so that most German Jews failed to recognize the direction of the Nazi policy and did not want to emigrate before 1938–1939? Was it really so obvious that emigration was the best choice, or for that matter, was it a real possibility for the

---

15 See Chapter 2.

majority of German Jews? On the other hand, can it be true that all those Jews, so faithful to their fatherland, all of a sudden were willing to embark on a hitherto neglected path, namely emigration? The following individual emigration decisions, their timing and destination choice before and after 1938 serve to address these questions.

Figure 6: Immigrants from Germany before embarking in Jaffa harbor, 1933. Courtesy of the Central Zionist Arvhives.

Emigration Decisions during the First Phase of the Nazi Regime

The first year of the Hitler regime witnessed upheaval of the wave related to the initial steps the Nazis took against Jewish and non-Jewish intellectuals and Jewish civil servants and professionals, and the boycott of Jewish business of 1 April, 1933. However, as soon as the initial overwhelming threat of the Nazi regime subsided a kind of semi-normalcy occurred, the flood turned, and the next upheaval of emigration would not occur before the year 1938.

On the whole, the majority of the early emigrants came from among those who lost their jobs and young students who could not see any professional future in Germany. As mentioned in Chapter 2, between 1933 and 1935 Palestine was the most accessible country for immigration.

It is clear that during the first years, especially 1933–1935, Palestine attracted a great proportion of the emigration from Germany, the trend moving opposite to the general rate of emigration. To what extent did it then play a role in decisions taken to immigrate? Of 45 autobiographical reports analyzed by Miron,[16] 24 belong to people who emigrated between 1933–1938. These people discussed here are by definition a select group of people with public and historical awareness, driven to write about their experiences with a sense of mission, and therefore they are not representative of the entire body of immigrants. Nevertheless, they exemplify some trends typical of early immigrants to Palestine. Their age at the time of immigration ranged between 20 and 57 years. Most of them were active Zionists – some Orthodox Jews – who held official positions in the state services as doctors, social workers and lawyers, and responded to being fired by immediate immigration to Palestine. For example, Alex Bein, born 1903, an archivist in Potsdam State Archives and an active Zionist, was fired and immigrated immediately afterwards to Jerusalem;[17] Werner Silberstein, born 1899, an Orthodox doctor and a Zionist, was fired from his position in the Prussian Institute for Infectious Diseases and immigrated in 1933;[18] Bertha Katz, born 1908, a social worker, was fired from the Institute for Children Welfare and moved with her family to Palestine in 1933.[19]

Others had to stop their studies or had already prepared for pioneering immigration to Palestine as members of *Kibbutz Hakhshara* (communal agricultural training group). This was the case with Shalom Ben-Chorin (Fritz Rosenthal), born 1913, a Zionist journalist and author, who was forced to stop his university studies and left for Palestine in 1935;[20] Asher Benari, born 1911, a student, joined a Zionist training farm following the Nazi seizure of power and immigrated with a group of pioneers who founded *Kibbutz* Hazore'a;[21] Drora Gafni (Hilda Weller) joined a German-Zionist *Hakhshara* in 1933 in Holland. In August 1935 she obtained an immigration certificate and went with her group to Palestine to establish a *kibbutz*.[22]

By and large, Zionism served as an infrastructure for them to make an early decision to immigrate. My own parents, Dr. Martin and Eva (nee Jeremias) Plessner present another example for abrupt decision. My father was fired from his position as a *Privatdozent* (untenured lecturer) in the University of Frankfurt and

---

16 Miron (2005).
17 Miron (2005), 306–307; Bein (1992).
18 Miron (2005), 309; Silberstein (1994).
19 Bertha Katz, Miron (2005), 310; Bertha Katz, "Autobiography," LBIANY, ME355.
20 Miron (2005), 307; Ben-Chorin (1974).
21 Miron (2005), 307; Benari (1986).
22 Dagan (2011).

had to emigrate if he wanted to pursue his academic career. Like many other young academics he considered crossing the border to Holland in order to establish himself in the international academic world before considering an overseas emigration, which in his case, as an ardent Zionist meant going to Palestine and joining the Hebrew University of Jerusalem, founded in 1925. Their chances were good to get immigration certificates to Palestine. They both grew up in Zionist families, and my mother's father, Karl Jeremias who died in 1914, was among the founders of the Zionist movement in Germany. However, in order to pursue an academic career the best option for my father seemed to first establish himself in his field of scholarship, and then, he hoped to be accepted by the young and small Hebrew University. My mother, on the other hand, did not opt for postponing immigration to Palestine; she was more radical, and argued that if leaving Germany is necessary in order to make a living, then the way should be directly to Palestine, which was their destination of choice anyway. Thus my father moved in April 1933 to find a job (he became a teacher in the Reali High School in Haifa), and my mother, with her father-in-law, followed suit half a year later.[23] Retrospectively, one could only imagine what would have happened if they had moved to Holland first, but no one could have foreseen the future war at that time.

But Zionism was only a part, not always decisive. Charlotte (Lotti) Steinberg (1908–2003), who completed her training as a dentist in 1934, saw no chance to pursue her career in Germany. She married a wealthy Jew and followed her Zionist husband to Palestine in 1935, where she could open her own private dental clinic in Tel Aviv.[24]

Britain, which introduced harsh anti-alien acts right after World War I,[25] could not, as opposed to Palestine, be considered a destination for most German Jews, unless they had some previous connections there, or belonged to the cultural and academic elite, for whom special arrangements were introduced by the establishment of the Academic Assistance Council to support immigration and absorption of German academics (AAC). The way was also opened for modern professionals in technology and industry, for whom there was a great demand in England. These factors may be illustrated by a few individual examples of early immigrants to Britain:

Lotte Hamburger's (nee Levy, born 1924) father had a hat factory and used skills unknown in Britain: he manufactured soft hats. Thus he had much

---

23 Personal testimonies given to the author by Martin Plessner (1900–1973) and Eva Plessner (1905–1991). See also: Levy (2016); Mendel (2016).

24 Boehling and Larkey (2011).

25 See Chapter 2.

business in exporting to England. In 1933, right after the boycott the family went to London.[26] Beatrice Musgrave, born 1924, grew up in Hamburg. Her father was a businessman and had lived in Bradford before World War I, and had relatives in England. Beatrice started to experience anti-Semitism at school and was sent in 1936 to a boarding school in Switzerland. Three weeks after her return to Hamburg the family immigrated to the U.K. in 1937.[27] Ellen Shiffman was born 1924 in Breslau, where she lived until 1930 when the family moved to Hamburg. Her brother was sent to a public school in England in 1935, and her parents began to look for somewhere to go. They visited Palestine but felt they could not live there since it was too underdeveloped. Through professional contacts her father, a physician, was sponsored to come to England in 1937/8. He went through all medical exams and sent for his wife and daughter. They arrived at the beginning of September 1938 and settled in Leicester.[28] Edith Bülbring was a hospital doctor in Berlin and eventually was fired after 1933. She went on a trip to London, where she met her former teacher who had already immigrated due to his good connections. He arranged for her to be interviewed for a job although she had not planned to immigrate. Since she was accepted she went back home and immediately thereafter immigrated to England.[29] Hans Grünberg was in his practical training as a hospital doctor in Freiburg when the Nazi came to power. Knowing that he would not be allowed to continue his career he intended to emigrate right after getting his diploma. Unexpectedly he received an invitation from Prof. Haldane of Cambridge, who was looking for young colleagues and got recommendations on his behalf.[30] Bernard Katz decided already before 1933 to complete his studies and to leave Germany. He finished his studies in 1934 and was introduced to Chaim Weizmann who helped him establish contact with the physiologist Prof. Hill, one of the founders of the AAC. Thereafter he arrived in England in 1935 with the help of relatives who lived in England.[31] Ludwig Spiro (born 1929) studied machine engineering, and immigrated to Britain in 1936, before completing his diploma, because there was a great demand for engineers.[32]

There were among the early immigrants to Britain those who came to study and did not consider immigration but stayed there anyway. Liselotte (Elisabeth Charlotte) Leschke was born in Berlin in 1914 to a Jewish mother and a non-Jewish

---

26 Personal interview, at the USHMM, Washington, D.C., 2005.
27 Refugee Voices, WLL, No. 86.
28 Refugee Voices, WLL, No. 16.
29 Imperial War Museum Sound Archives, London (hereafter: IWM), no. 004532/02.
30 IWM Sound Archives No. 004478.
31 IWM Sound Archives, No.004508.
32 IWM Sound Archives, No. 004343.

father, both academics. Liselotte was educated as a thoroughly assimilated child unaware of anti-Semitism in Hamburg. She left Germany for Britain in 1933 to study English, intending to become an interpretor, and became a student teacher at Badminton School, Bristol.[33] Ingrid Heichelheim, born in Breslau 1919 into a musical family, came to Britain in 1936 as an au pair, took singing lessons at the Royal College of Music and resolved to stay.[34] Max Milner was born in Berlin in 1918. In June 1936 he was sent to Aryeh House, a Jewish boarding school in Brighton, where he matriculated in January 1937. He returned to Berlin and in September 1937 he enrolled in Edinburgh University to study engineering. The rest of his family immigrated to Palestine.[35]

On the whole, the above cases mirror the tiny number of German immigrants who came to England before 1938, many of them due to former connections or with organized assistance on behalf of scientists and industrialists. Most of them came from the upper middle class, were young and able to start or continue their studies or to embark on an early career.

Immigrants to the U.S.A. in the early period – who were not among the great number of intellectuals and scientists who were summoned to immigrate,[36] were – like their compatriots who went to England – connected to the U.S.A. Here a sequential or chain migration was a central factor. The case of Marianne Steinberg (1911–2002) represents the thought process with the choice of destination, as late as 1938, and illustrates the role of a possible chain migration. When Hitler came to power she was in the middle of her medical studies and was forced to complete her studies and submit her dissertation in Switzerland. Marianne was adamant about completing her diploma against all odds, before emigration. She started to consider emigration during her studies and pondered the possibilities. Palestine was then, in the beginning of 1936, still attractive, and her sister Lotti was there and offered her help, eager that Marianne join her, but on the other hand, the country already had a surplus of doctors following the great influx from Germany, and it was not easy anymore to enter the quota. America – and particularly New York that did not require an additional examination in order to obtain a hospital position – had advantages for absorbing physicians, and her boyfriend was already there. In the meantime, the situation in Germany worsened and her family voted for the U.S.A., considering the possibility to immigrate later on with the help of Marianne who would by then be settled and able to support an

---

33 Refugee Voices, WLL, No. 29.
34 Refugee Voices, WLL, No. 9.
35 Refugee Voices, WLL, No. 3.
36 More details in Chapter 5.

affidavit. Marianne decided in early 1938 to go to America. She obtained an affidavit from distant relatives and friends and arrived in New York in June 1938.[37]

In some cases the possibility of a chain migration made itself available due to young German Jews who had immigrated to the U.S.A. during the Weimar period. This was the case with Siegfried Rosenthal, born 1908. After Hitler came to power, his parents travelled to the U.S.A. to visit their adult children, whom they had not seen for the last seven years. The children convinced them to stay, and they crossed the border to Canada to obtain immigrant visas. Siegfried and his sister then quickly decided to follow their parents.[38] Maria Munk was a lawyer and an active feminist who came to Chicago to participate in the International Congress of Women, sponsored by the National Council of Women of the United States in July 1933. She was welcomed by her nephew who had settled in New York already in 1924, and she was also very impressed by the highly professional American welfare institutions. Thus, she decided to immediately immigrate and did so, with her family, in April 1934.[39] Alfred Mayer was confronted by Nazism in school already in 1932 and after searching for possibilities to continue studies abroad received an affidavit from his aunt in the U.S.A. and in 1935 arrived in New York.[40]

The case of Walter Heinemann represents the complexity of escaping and the role of chances regarding destinations. Heinemann, born 1883, a doctor in the public health insurance system, was fired and arrested in April 1933. Already after the burning of the Reichstag in February 1933 he realized that this was not going to change for the better and arranged for a passport. When he received it he travelled to Holland to arrange through his brother-in-law a meeting with the British consul in Berlin, who advised him to start getting the sum of 1,000 Pounds required for a visa for Palestine.[41] After the issue of the Nuremberg Laws in 1935 the consul granted him a visa and he went to Palestine with his mother, leaving his wife in England. "I went to Palestine as a non-Zionist because at that time there was no other possibility... But then I went on because I didn't find there a possibility to establish myself." At the age of 55 he found it too difficult to adjust and after six months he went to England to meet with his wife, realizing that the only possibility would be to go to the U.S. He had no relatives who could obtain an affidavit on his behalf, so he went to the consul and put his case bluntly before

---

37 Boehling and Larkey (2011).

38 Testimony by Siegfried Rosenthal, LBIANY, ME 962 MM II 21.

39 Testimony by Maria Munk, LBIANY, ME 332 MM 127.

40 Testimony by Alfred Mayer, LBIANY, ME 236.

41 This was apparently Captain Francis Edward Foley, the person in charge of visa allocation in the British consulate, hailed for his generosity and flexibility by the head of the emigration department of the *Hilfsverein der Deutschen Juden*. See Ball-Kaduri (1967); Smith (1999).

him. The consul was obviously impressed and after a while decided to grant a visa without an affidavit. He arrived in New York in June 1936 and his wife followed suit in September, after he had completed his medical examinations.[42]

In general it seems that most – but not all – early immigrants came from among academics and professionals, who could transfer their skills free from the dilemmas of industrialists and business persons who hesitated to abandon a growing share of their assets and start anew abroad without their capital base. It seems also that most of the early emigrants belonged to the younger generation, as is the case with any mass migration.[43] However, the cases given above may indicate that there were many exceptions and different types of emigrants whose decisions were motivated rather by the pull factors of the different destinations. Moreover, many cases signify the role of chance that caused unpremeditated migration, such as employment or study opportunities, connections abroad and occasional travels. By and large, all these were pull factors. Thus, it is quite obvious that during the years preceding 1938 German-Jewish emigrants were not refugees in the full meaning of the term, at least not from their own subjective perspectives. They still calculated their emigration, its timing and destination, and did not feel forced to emigrate by all means.

Late Emigration – after *Kristallnacht*

Crucial factors in this late emigration wave were the changing policies of the U.S. and Britain as a consequence of the November pogrom. This turning point enabled German Jews to flee Germany at all cost, as refugees. By this time it was not anymore a matter of choice if, when, and where to immigrate, but to grasp every possible opportunity. But this did not mean that they started only then to consider emigration. Many of those fleeing now after *Kristallnacht* had considered earlier emigration and tried to leave Germany before November 1938, but only following these events did they manage to acquire the necessary permits thanks to the impact of their plight on the eased immigration policies of the U.S. and Britain. Emigration from Germany was dependent to a large degree on possibilities, and *Kristallnacht* affected immigration policies in the U.S. and Britain at least as much as it drove Jews to flee Germany. Without a change in the American and British immigration policies, the mass emigration following November 1938 could not have happened.

A few individual examples will demonstrate this. Carl Schwabe from Hanau near Frankfurt started to think about immigration to Palestine in 1935, but the

---

42 Testimony of Walter Heinemann, LBIANY, ME 284.
43 Barkai (1989), 100; Niederland (1996), 70–71.

dim economic prospects prevented him from doing so. He then applied for an American visa, started to study English and waited, but he was arrested in the eve of *Kristallnacht*. When he was released, the process of finally getting a visa had been accelerated, and he soon immigrated with his wife to the U.S.[44]

In other cases, people were too afraid of the difficulties of emigrating, and thought that time would allow them to postpone it. This was the case with Rudolf Bing. He wanted to join his two daughters who had already immigrated to Palestine in 1933. However, as the Chair of the Palestine Office in Nuremberg and a legal counselor, he felt compelled to help his fellow Jews who were trapped between the intensifying terror and the obstacles created by preventive Nazi regulations regarding currency, taxation, and the possibilities of exporting capital. Only the pogrom forced him to flee, and he eventually arrived in Palestine.[45]

Others who did not understand the deteriorating situation in Germany until 1938 nevertheless acted even before *Kristallnacht*. Ernst Loewenberg, a teacher in an experimental left-wing school in Hamburg, enjoyed the loyalty and friendship of his German colleagues, and even after he was forced to leave the school and to become a teacher in a Jewish religious school (*Talmud Tora*), he did not consider emigration. When he applied at last in August 1938 for an American visa, his non-Jewish friends were surprised. He was lucky and arrived in the U.S. in November 1938.[46]

And there were those who indeed were actually forced to emigrate in November 1938 and barely managed to do so. Charlotte Levy's father was arrested in November 1938 and applied for an American visa, but since there was a long waiting list, her parents decided to send her alone in the *Kindertransport* to England.[47] Shmuel Kneller, born in 1925, remembers that upon returning to school 14 days after the pogrom, he realized that many classmates were missing – their fathers had been arrested and were released only on condition that they leave Germany.[48]

Hilde (Anker) Fogelson, born on May 29, 1926 in Berlin, was the daughter of Georg and Gertrud Anker. She had two older sisters, Eva (b. 1922) and Dodi (b. 1924). Gertrud and Georg sent their three daughters, Eva, Dodi and Hilde, to England with a *Kindertransport* that arrived on June 14, 1939. On July 13, 1939 Georg and Gertrud flew to Copenhagen, where they stayed briefly before joining

---

44 Testimony of Carl Schwabe, LBIANY, ME 586, MM 68.

45 Testimony of Rudolf Bing, LBIANY, ME 267, MM 10.

46 Testimony of Ernst Loewenberg, LBIANY, ME 403, MM 51.

47 Testimony of Charlotte Levy, in: Marßolek and Davids (1997): 141–147.

48 Lecture by Shmuel Kneller on 9 November, 2008, in Haifa, author's personal collection.

their daughters in England. In October 1940 the Anker family sailed to the United States aboard the SS Nova Scotia.[49]

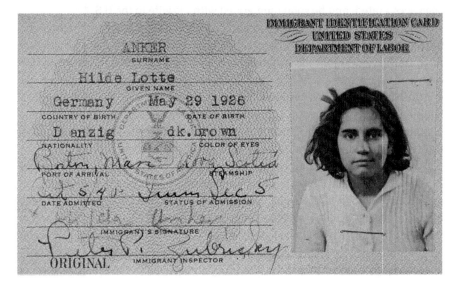

Figure 7: Immigrant identification card issued to the German Jewish refugee child, Hilde Anker, upon her arrival in Boston in October 1940. Courtesy of the U.S. Holocaust Memprial Museum.

Most of those who tried to seek refuge before or after the pogrom were trying to reach the U.S.A. However, they faced a huge obstacle in getting an affidavit (this was the indispensable condition for getting a visa, even after entering the quota waiting list), namely to find a sponsor.

In order to get a sponsor one had to preferably have a relative who was not only willing but financially capable of totally supporting the new immigrants for a full year. The Lichtenstein family from Breslau had an immigration number and, in March 1938, Mr. Lichtenstein tried to get an affidavit from his aunt in Detroit, Michigan. He went to America for that purpose but it didn't work out. While en route he was fortunate to meet an American citizen, Sally Bloom, who was returning home to New York from a family visit in Rumania. She heard his story and offered an affidavit in case the aunt could not supply it. Indeed the aunt could not supply it, and the Bloom family became the sponsor who enabled

---

49 United States Holocaust Memorial Museum, courtesy of George Fogelson (Collections: 2003.353, text accompanying photo 15286).

Mr. Lichtenstein to bring his wife and two children, who reached New York a year later, in March 1939.[50]

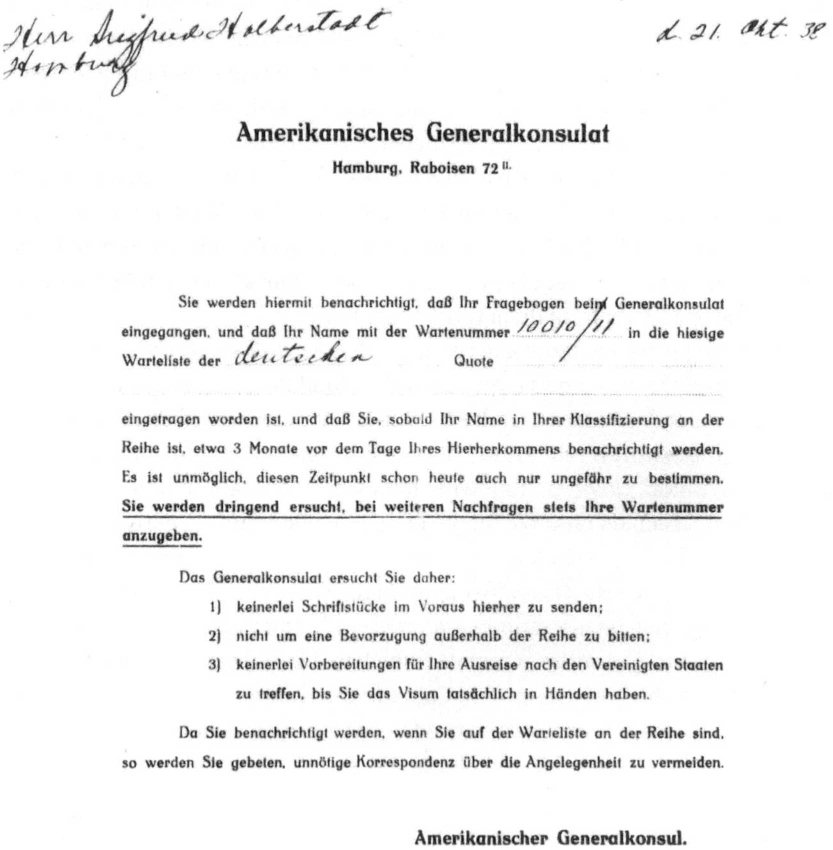

Herr Siegfried Halberstadt Hamburg   *d. 21. Okt. 38*

Amerikanisches Generalkonsulat

Hamburg, Raboisen 72 II.

Sie werden hiermit benachrichtigt, daß Ihr Fragebogen beim Generalkonsulat eingegangen, und daß Ihr Name mit der Wartenummer *10010/11* in die hiesige Warteliste der *deutschen* Quote

eingetragen worden ist, und daß Sie, sobald Ihr Name in Ihrer Klassifizierung an der Reihe ist, etwa 3 Monate vor dem Tage Ihres Hierherkommens benachrichtigt werden. Es ist unmöglich, diesen Zeitpunkt schon heute auch nur ungefähr zu bestimmen. **Sie werden dringend ersucht, bei weiteren Nachfragen stets Ihre Wartenummer anzugeben.**

Das Generalkonsulat ersucht Sie daher:

1) keinerlei Schriftstücke im Voraus hierher zu senden;
2) nicht um eine Bevorzugung außerhalb der Reihe zu bitten;
3) keinerlei Vorbereitungen für Ihre Ausreise nach den Vereinigten Staaten zu treffen, bis Sie das Visum tatsächlich in Händen haben.

Da Sie benachrichtigt werden, wenn Sie auf der Warteliste an der Reihe sind, so werden Sie gebeten, unnötige Korrespondenz über die Angelegenheit zu vermeiden.

Amerikanischer Generalkonsul.

Figure 8: Document sent by the American consulate in Hamburg to Siegfried Halberstadt, informing him of his number on the waiting list of Germans seeking visas to immigrate to the United States, October 21, 1938. Courtesy of the U.S. Holocaust Memorial Museum.

There were other complicated ways in which people pursued a search to find distant relatives. It sometimes helped and sometimes failed. Jacob Mann from Nuremberg succeeded in late October 1938 to find a cousin he had never known before in a process of trial and error, based on research in the family's old correspondence.

---

50 USHMM Archives, RG 19/017/01 (Story of Sally and Samuel Bloom).

He was assisted by the National Council of Jewish Women to locate and contact his cousins Sidney and Morris Mandelbaum in Des Moines, Iowa. The cousins agreed in coordination with the National Coordinating Committee for Aid to Refugees and Emigrants Coming from Germany (that recruited sponsors and coordinated their support for refugees). By July 1939 Jacob Mann and his wife received a permit to sojourn in England (based on the British agreement to accept temporarily refugees holding affidavits who were on the waiting list for American visas), to join their daughter Lily, who had already arrived there on a separate American affidavit. By December 1939 the Mann family had already been settled in London, assisted by the local German-Jewish Aid Committee. In August 1940 the Mann family reached the shores of New York. The fate of other family members – old cousins of Jacob Mann – was apparently sealed. They started to look for an affidavit in 1939 with no avail, and the last heard from them was 5 June, 1941.[51]

There were also a few thousand refugees after *Kristallnacht* who ended up in Palestine within the very limited quotas of the Mandate government which gave priority to German Jews. Kurt Steinberg (1906–1969) was trained as a lawyer and worked with the *Centralverein*. He did not consider leaving his old mother and her sister for emigration. However, following his sister's emigration to the U.S. in the middle of 1938 it seemed possible for the family to follow suit. In early September 1938 he did at last register in the American consulate. He got a number between 19,000–20,000. During the November pogrom he was arrested and imprisoned in Buchenwald and was released upon a promise of his employer at the CV that he would immigrate to Argentina, a promise which was based on false papers. In the very last moment the British consul in Cologne gave him and his fiancée a tourist certificate to Palestine, where they arrived in early 1939 as a married couple.[52]

Two cases of older people, who planned to emigrate but did not succeed, not even following the November pogrom, may serve to conclude this chapter.

Selma Kaufmann-Steinberg (1871–1942), a widow by the time Hitler came to power, lived and owned with her unmarried sister Henriette (Henny, 1875–1942) a small business in Altenessen. All of her three children had already emigrated, two to Palestine, and one to the U.S. Selma and her sister, who became ill, did not consider emigration even though Selma visited her daughter Lotti in 1937 in Tel Aviv, and Lotti tried to persuade her to stay. After the Munich conference she wrote to her daughter Marianne in the U.S.: "Thank God the difficult and worrisome days have finally passed." She started to think about emigration in the fall of 1938, following her son Kurt's registering for immigration to the U.S. in October 1938.

---

51 USHMM Archives, RG 19/016 (Mandelbaum Family Correspondence).
52 Boehling and Larkey (2011).

Her registration number was 31,691– unlikely to be able to immigrate for several years. When she registered the main concern of her daughters in Tel Aviv and New York was to get her to safety with their brother Kurt who had been arrested and forced to emigrate. The proceeds from the family's property sales, along with the relative calm in Germany and the recent avoidance of war created an illusion that the old folks would be safe while waiting in Germany until the children could get fully settled. Thus, Lotti submitted a request to bring her mother to Palestine only in April 1939. By then this was not likely to happen, due to the changing Mandatory government's immigration policy.[53]

Auswanderung

הגירה

überfahrt Febr. 1939

Februar 1939 an bord der „SS Jerusalemme" nach Palestina.

Figure 9: The newly wed Steinbergs on the boat to Palestine, February 1939. Courtesy of Miryam Shomrat and Gideon Sela.

---

53 Boehling and Larkey (2011).

The couple Weller, whose daughter had immigrated to Palestine in 1935, already then had begun to inquire regarding the possibility to follow her, on the condition that she would not feel compelled to leave the *kibbutz* in order to support them. The British Mandate regulations regarding parents of residents or recent immigrants were very complicated and depended on what the estimated impact of the middle-aged parents on the economy was, or what the chances of the residents to support them were. Members of newly established *kibbutzim* (plural of *kibbutz*) were in the worst position and were not counted as being able to guarantee the wellbeing of their parents. On the other hand, in times of recession, middle-aged people could not receive certificates as labor seekers.[54] In October 1938 Ernst Weller became more optimistic: "Now, after the Munich agreement the risk of war fades away and the British might return to a solution of the Arab-Jewish conflict and revise their immigration regulations." A few days later he expressed his hopes that he would soon cross the age barrier of 55 and be allowed to enter Palestine as a dependent who does not pose a burden on the labor market. Then came the November pogrom, and he was arrested and imprisoned in Dachau, and like others was released on the condition that he emigrate immediately. Many relatives of the Wellers immigrated to the U.S., but the Wellers were so confident that their destiny was to join their daughter in Palestine, and they focused on this option alone. But this was not meant to be. Only after the war did the daughter find out that they had been deported and murdered.[55]

A similar case was that of Willy Cohn from Breslau, born in 1888, a liberal religious German historian and teacher, who was also a supporter of Zionism. He encouraged his son to immigrate to Palestine and later his daughter to join a training farm and to follow the same route. In 1937 he pondered the idea to go to Palestine and went there with his second wife Trudi for a long visit and tour. However, there was no chance for him to find employment and his wife opposed the idea. She tried to persuade him to try the American way instead but he resisted. At the age of 50 years he was the father of two very young daughters and could not think of emigrating without any prospect and connections. Palestine was for him an exception, an unfulfilled dream and he would not leave his beloved country. On 21 November, 1941, Willy Cohn, his wife Trudi, and their two daughters, Susanne, 9 years old, and Tamara, 3 years old, were deported with a thousand Jews from Breslau. Only recently it was discovered that they were shot to death in Kovno on 29 November, together with hundreds of Jews from Kovno and Germany.[56]

---

54 For discussion of this component in the Mandate immigration regulations see Halamish (2006), 292–301.
55 Dagan (2011).
56 Cohn (2014).

Of the 170,000 Jews still in Germany when the war broke out, 32 percent were over 60 years old, and more than a half were over 50. Selma and her sister, the Wellers and the Cohns were among those who did not survive, despite the emigration of their children who tried to get them out and could not imagine that any postponement meant a death sentence. In all these cases, the younger generation learned about their old folks' fate only after the war, and carried in their hearts the burden of guilt that they had not managed to get them out on time. This sense of guilt – just like the tendency to blame the Jews themselves for being blind and for clinging to their German fatherland – was built upon the false assumption created retrospectively, as if they could and should have imagined what would happen, and as if they could have worked against the huge odds put in their way by those in power, in and outside of Germany.

In Conclusion

German-Jewish interwar overseas emigration may be divided into three periods.

In the first, the Weimar era emigration was motivated mainly by economic push factors. During that period, the U.S.A. was the chief destination and the new 1924 quota system did not affect Germany. At the same time Palestine emerged as a new favored destination, especially for young people who were also motivated by ideological Zionism.

The second period – 1933–1938 – was marked by two major changes – the Nazi persecution as a push factor, and Palestinian prosperity – until 1935 – as a pull factor. By that time Palestine had taken the lead as a receiving immigration country. German Jews were only 20 percent of the many immigrants – the majority of them Polish – who reached Palestine in this period. However, at this time the U.S. and practically the rest of the world was almost closed for Jewish immigration, including the German Jews.

The third period started in the year 1938 with the intensifying danger to Central European Jews especially after the *Kristallnacht* pogrom. This period saw a huge wave of emigration that was by all standards a refugee emigration not only in hindsight but also from the perspective of the participants themselves, migrants and governments of the major destinations overseas. As such, this was not a select group motivated by pull factors, but a group of those fortunate people who were rescued by foreign governments, even though no one could have foreseen the dreadful fate of those who stayed behind.

This argument is clearly illustrated in looking at the proportion of the German-Jewish migration within the total Jewish interwar immigration to the three main overseas destinations. During the Weimar era the proportion of German-Jewish migrants was negligible to both Palestine and the U.S., despite the possibilities in both destinations, notwithstanding the adoption of immigration restrictions in the U.S., on the one hand, and the opening of Palestine, on the other. This testifies to the fact that the push factors – which are considered decisive in creating mass migration – were very weak. During these years the main source of Jewish migration was Poland, and due to the new immigration policy of 1921 Palestine became their main destination. During the first half of the Nazi era the situation in Germany changed dramatically. Now strong push factors in Germany came into the play, while Palestine became the most open destination. Polish Jews were still struggling to reach the only destination open to them. The U.S., under pressure of the economic crisis, in practice ceased to play the role of receiving country, and together with Britain allowed only a few thousand German Jews to enter. In the last period, 1936–1939, due to the change in the Palestine Mandate policy, the pressure on the U.S. and Britain mounted; only from late 1938 on did they respond to the plight of German Jews as an exception to their general restrictive immigration policies. Actually these responses made it possible for German Jews to immigrate in the latter period before the war, and it is clear that they made up the bulk of the Jewish immigration to both countries, in particular to Britain.

It should be emphasized that beyond those managing to reach these three destinations legally, there were also those who managed to enter their destination illegally. However it is quite impossible to estimate their numbers in general, or to assess the German-Jewish share in the estimated total, in particular. In the case of Palestine the estimated total number of illegal immigrants before the war was some 20,000.[57] The total number for the U.S. during the decades the quotas were in force is probably numbered in the tens of thousands, a relatively small number.[58]

Table 7: German-Jewish proportion of the interwar Jewish immigration to Palestine, the U.S.A. and Britain (total numbers in thousands)

Period	To Palestine				To the U.S.A.				To Britain			
	Total		German		Total		German		Total		German	
	No.	%	No.	%	No.	%	No.	%	No.	%	No.	%
1920–31	115	100	3	3	360	100	7	2				
1932–35	161	100	31	19	14	100	10	71	4	100	4	100
1936–39	86	100	27	31	81	100	72	89	83	100	83	100
1920–39	362	100	61	17	455	100	89	20	87	100	87	100

Sources: Calculation based on the data sources for Tables 2, 4, 5, 6 above.

---

57 For Palestine: Sicron (1957), 19, Table 3.
58 Garland (2014), 145.

Figure 10: Group portrait of German Jews en route to the United States on board the President Harding. Nov. 1939. Courtesy of the U.S. Holocaust Memorial Museum.

Figure 11: A Jewish refugee family from Germany poses for a picture as their ship, the SS Rotterdam, arrives in New York harbor, 1939. Courtesy of the U.S. Holocaust Memorial Museum.

During this last period, another significant phenomenon was the dispersion of the German-Jewish refugees to all corners of the world. Latin American countries – including in addition to Argentina and Brazil, also Bolivia, Chile, Colombia, Cuba, Ecuador, Mexico, Paraguay, Peru, and Uruguay– became the destination for some 75,000 German and Austrian Jews who in many cases entered without valid visas, circumventing immigration restrictions.[59] The British Dominions were also reached by refugees despite immigration restrictions. South Africa was reached by about 6,000 Jews from Central Europe; Canada and Australia by 4,000 each, and Shanghai became the home for some 8,000 refugees.[60]

Table 8: Dispersion of German-Jewish emigration around the World, 1920–1939

U.S.A.	Britan	Palestie	Latin* America	British** Dominions	Shanghi	total
89,000	87,000	61,000	75,000***	14,000***	8,000***	334,000***
27 %	26 %	18 %	22 %	4 %	2 %	100 %

* Including: Argentina, Bolivia, Brazil, Chile, Colombia, Cuba, Ecuador, Mexico, Paraguay, Peru, and Uruguay.
** Including Australia, Canada, South Africa.
*** Estimations refer sometimes to all Central Europeans. Most estimations relate to the years 1938 and after and include the war years.

---

59 Estimation based on Strauss (1981), 363–382.
60 Strauss (1981), 384–389.

Chapter 5
Demographic and Occupational Profile of the Immigrants

Palestine

The Weimar Era

Among the Jews emigrating from Germany during the Weimar era, some 3,300 immigrated to Palestine. The last chapter discussed the push factors determining the choice of timings and destinations by various groups of emigrants. Those immigrating to Palestine were young Zionists, mainly students abandoning academic studies or deciding to acquire new skills appropriate for immigration to Palestine.

The demographical and occupational structure of this group upon arrival is shown in Table 9.

Table 9: Demographic and occupational structure of German-Jewish immigrants to Palestine 1923–1924 (about 500 immigrants, in %)

Marital status	%	Occupational Structure (80 % of Immigrants)	%
Unmarried	71.4	Professionals	31.1
Married	24.5	Agriculture	28.7
Unknown	4.1	Craftmen	26.6
		Merchants	13.6
Total	100.0	Total earners	100.0

Source for data: CZA, S6/4878, S4/16, S4/26/1.

The figures reported in Table 9 point to the distinctive socio-economic attributes of this group of German immigrants. It was made up of young, unmarried, educated and professionally trained people. A significant number of the immigrants were active members of Zionist organizations, which prepared them professionally – either as individuals or in groups – for the needs of Palestine and for the requisition of immigration certificates.

DOI 10.1515/9783110501650-006

The Nazi Era

Following Hitler's seizure of power in January 1933, the wave of emigration started immediately. During the first three years that followed, the proportion of immigration to Palestine was about a third, and Palestine took priority among overseas destinations (see Chapter 4, Table 4). The following table reflects the changing proportion of Palestine as a destination and its decline against the growing flood of emigration from Germany toward the end of the 1930s.

Table 10: The proportion of immigrants to Palestine within the total Jewish emigration from Germany, 1933–1939, by year

Year	From Germany (100%)	To Palestine	
		Numbers	Percent
1933	37,000	7,200	19.5
1934	23,000	9,400	41.0
1935	21,000	7,900	37.6
1936	25,000	8,400	33.6
1937	23,000	3,500	15.2
1938	40,000	6,900	17.2
1939	126,000	8,500	6.7
1933–1939	226,000	51,800	22.9

Sources: Traub (1936); Joint Reports, 1936, 1937, 1938, YIVO; JA (1939); Barkai (1997), 227; Gelber (1990), 57.

Age Composition

Table 11 below reflects the high proportion – almost 30 percent – of children and youth (age 1–20 years) among the German immigrants to Palestine, which signifies that many immigrants came as young families. The proportion of the over 50 years old was remarkably small – 12 percent – and the rate of adults (21–50) capable of working was over 50 percent, of whom the majority – 41 percent of the total – were young adults under 40 years of age. These proportions did not represent the aging profile of German Jewry. The high proportion of young adults is also linked with British Mandate immigration policy, limiting allocation of labor certificates directly or via the JA to those aged 17–35 and in good health. During the second half of the 1930s, older people, even parents of local residents were particularly restricted from entering Mandatory Palestine. The high percentage of children and youth was also due to the Youth *Aliya* project that brought about 5,000 children under the age of 17 years between 1934–1939.[1]

---

1 See Chapter 2.

Table 11: Age composition of the immigrants from Germany to Palestine, 1933–1938 (numbers in thousands)

Year/Age	Total		1–9		10–20		21–30		31–40		41–50		51 +	
	%		%		%		%		%		%		%	
1933	7.2	100	1.1	15	1.0	14	1.7	24	1.6	22	0.7	10	0.4	
1934	9.4	100	1.0	11	1.6	17	2.6	28	1.7	18	0.7	9	0.8	
1935	7.9	100	0.7	8	1.3	17	2.4	30	1.3	17	0.7	10	1.1	
1936	8.4	100	0.6	7	1.9	23	2.2	26	1.1	13	0.8	10	1.3	
1937	3.5	100	0.2	7	0.7	19	1.0	29	0.5	14	0.3	10	0.6	
1938	6.9	100	0.4	6	2.1	30	1.0	14	0.8	12	0.7	11	1.2	
Total	43.3	100	4.0	9	8.6	20	10.9	25	7.0	16	3.9	10	5.4	12

Source: Based on Gelber (1990), 59.

Marital Status, Family, and Gender

A statistical survey of the German immigrants who entered Palestine through the ports of Haifa and Tel Aviv reveals the following:

Table 12: Marital status and family composition of the German immigrants to Palestine 1933–1939

	1933	1934	1935	1936	1937	1938*	1939*	Total	
								No.	%
Heads of family	1,455	1,912	1,652	1,635	816	1,277	1,924	10,671	
Family Members	4,405	5,419	4,292	4,341	2,062	3,394	5,038	28,951	62
Average family size								3	
Singles**	2,114	3,078	3,165	3,566	1,218	2,744	3,836	17,821	38
Total	6,519	8,497	7,457	7,907	3,380	6,138	8,874	46,772	100

Calculation based on data of: Report on immigration from Germany (1939), CZA, S25/2333.
* Data for the years 1938–1939 include immigrants from Austria.
** Including children who came as singles (Youth *Aliya*).

On the whole it is apparent that about two thirds of the immigrants came as families throughout the period. The average size of a family was three persons and there were probably many couples without children. As for the gender composition – the proportion of males was just slightly higher than females (54 percent) because among the singles the proportion of males was much higher.[2]

---

2 Based on the report at CZA, S25/2333 (see source for Table 12).

Occupational Structure

In a striking contradiction to the occupational structure of Jews in Germany, 34 percent of the German-Jewish immigrants to Palestine in the 1930s were active bread winners. Since most were heads or chief provider of families, the total percentage of those living on an active economic occupation amounted to 73 percent of the immigrants, as seen in Table 13:

Table 13: Occupational status of immigrants from Germany to Palestine, 1933–1939

Occupational Status	Number	Percent
Total Breadwinners	14,652	33.7
Not mentioned*	14,507	33.4
Students	2,563	5.9
Children	11,772	27.0
Total	43,494	100.0

Source: Calculation based on data of: Report on immigration from Germany (1939), CZA, S25/2333.
Data for the years 1938–1939 include immigrants from Austria.
* Mainly women homemakers who were not considered breadwinners.

The occupational structure was also quite different from that typifying the German-Jewish population at the time. Among the occupations there were about 16 percent of those who already had worked in agriculture (mainly on training farms), and the percentage of those who were living in Germany working in commercial activity was significantly lower than the proportion typical to German Jewry, as is manifested in Table 14:

Table 14: Occupational structure of the immigrants from Germany to Palestine, 1933–1939

Occupation	Number	Percent of Total Breadwinners
Agriculture	2,374	16.3
Industry	3,570	24.4
Free Professions	3,109*	21.2
Commerce	4,151	28.3
Clerks	719	4.8
Laborers	729	5.0
Total Breadwinners	14,652	100.0

Source: Calculation based on data of: Report on immigration from Germany (1939), CZA, S25/2333.
Data for the years 1938–1939 include immigrants from Austria.
*The main fields: medicine (9 percent), education/academia (3.5 percent), law (3.2 percent).

Early immigrants from Nazi Germany could bring with them their capital and, indeed, some 19,900 immigrants entered the country as "capitalists," declaring the possession of minimum 1,000 pounds, namely 31 percent of the 52,500 German immigrants.

The U.S.A.

The Weimar Era

The chief destination for Jews and non-Jews alike from the business and commerce strata was the U.S.A.[3] The 7,700 Jews who are estimated to have arrived in the U.S.A. during the 1920s came thus mainly from their ranks – the sons of businessmen who saw no future in Germany.[4] Although there exist little available data, it is estimated that they were mainly young people and probably many of them arrived alone to begin their careers in the new country.

The Nazi Era

Only partial data are available relating specifically to immigrating German Jews as distinct from Germans on the one hand and from "Hebrews" (those registered as Jews in general) on the other. There is also a dearth of data distinguishing between Germany and Austria. Between 1933 and 1941 the United States granted immigrant visas to 129,600 people from Germany and Austria.[5] These accounted for more than a quarter of the 500,000 refugees fleeing from Nazi ruled Central Europe.[6] Of the Germans and Austrians, 81,500 (or 68 percent) were self-identified as Jews by religion.[7] According to Davie and Koenig, a majority of the remainder were so-called "non-Aryan Christians," namely, Jews by racial descent according to the Nazi definition, who were not characterized as "Hebrews" by U.S. immigration authorities.[8]

---

3 Lavsky (1987).
4 Malina (1931).
5 Davie and Koenig (1945), 7–9.
6 Krohn (1998).
7 HIAS figure of 81,500 in YIVO Archives, RG 245.4.5, MF 15.12 V-I, II: Table titled "Jewish Immigrant Aliens Admitted from July 1st 1933 to June 30, 1943 by Last Permanent Residence, Including Austria from 1937/8."
8 Davie and Koenig (1945). In his later book Davie wrote that the number of Jews arriving in the United States between 1933 and 1944 who were born in Germany was 97,374; see Davie (1947). Another estimation of the total (Jewish and non-Jewish) German immigration, excluding Austria, during the years 1933–1941 quotes a figure of 104,000: see Kent (1953); Jay (1997).

Between February 1933 and March 1936, the U.S. received only 9,500 of the total of 93,000 emigrants from Germany.[9] The majority of the Central European immigrants (both Jews and non-Jews) entered the U.S. from the end of 1938 onward. Those who immigrated earlier were almost exclusively from Germany, and they came in moderate numbers, rising from 1,200 in 1933 to about 12,000 in 1937. With the arrival of 18,000 additional newcomers by the middle of 1938, German immigrants totaled about 46,000,[10] of whom more than half (about 27,000) were estimated to be Jews.[11]

According to U.S. immigration quotas as amended in 1929, it was legally possible to admit 25,557 German immigrants per year. Until 1938–1939, the quota was not filled, both because of the many rules limiting the categories of those eligible for a visa, and because of various bureaucratic obstacles put into practice by the American consulate in Berlin. This situation changed in the wake of the events of 1938, which took such a toll on German and Austrian Jews. Although the quota laws were not altered, a new category – Refugees – was introduced, and this circumvented many of the existing limitations and obstacles in granting visas.[12]

Table 15: The proportion of immigrants to the U.S.A. within the total Jewish emigration from Germany in selected periods

Period	From Germany*	To the U.S.A.	
	Total in thousands	in thousands	% of total
1933–1935	93	9.5**	10.2
1933–1938	169	27***	16.0
1938–1941	141	55****	39.0
1933–1941	270	82*****	30.4

* Data in Table 5, above.
** Traub (1936)1936, based on official German sources.
*** Davie and Koenig (1945), 14–15.
**** Based on HIAS material, YIVO Archives, RG 245.4.5 MF 15.12 V-I, II: Table "Jewish immigrant aliens admitted from July 1st 1933 to June 30 1943, by last permanent residence, including Austria from 1937/8."
***** Ibid., amended by adding half the number of the previous fiscal year to cover calendar years. Though Austria is included it is estimated that immigrants from Austria constituted only a small minority in the numbers cited.

---

9 Traub (1936), 10–11, 14–17.
10 Based on Joseph Perkins Chamberlain's tables in the Chamberlain Collection, YIVO Archives (YIVO), RG 278, Box 4; *Refugee Facts* (1939). The tabulation of immigrant entries according to the U.S. fiscal year at that time (July-June) effectively extends the estimate of a given calendar year into the first six months of the next calendar year, and this affects the estimate.
11 Rosenstock (1956), 376; Strauss (1978), xx.
12 Zucker (2001), 36–48.

During the period 1933–1935, the United States received slightly more than 10 percent of the German-Jewish emigration; through 1938, the total was 16 percent. In 1938, 40,000 Jews left Germany. The exodus intensified after the *Kristallnacht* pogrom, when U.S.-bound immigrants accounted for a major share of the total: between 1938 and 1941, some 55,000 Jewish refugees from Germany and Austria entered the United States.[13]

Demographic and Socio-Economic Profile of the Immigrants

Analyzing the profiles of the immigrants from Nazi Germany to the U.S.A., the post-1938 influx can undoubtedly be considered a refugee migration, as reflected by the high proportion of older adults as compared with the arrivals of 1933–1938 (see Table 16), indicating the lack of age selectivity among the Jewish immigrants in the latter years. However, since the size of the later wave of German refugees was by far larger than the trickle of earlier immigrants, and since it was now accompanied by great numbers of refugees from countries other than Germany, the whole immigration stream of the 1930s can be characterized as refugee migration. As such it was indeed different from former immigration waves and included larger proportion of women, children and adults aged 45 years and over. The proportion of children was slightly affected by the special government grant of 1,000 visas for unaccompanied children in 1939.[14]

Table 16: Demographic and socio-economic profile of the immigrants to the U.S.A. during the 1930s, in percentages

Age	% 1933–38	% 1938–41	Occupation	Percent
0–20	30	18	Business	58.5
21–50	55	51	Industry	3.5
51+	15	31	Professions	38.0
Total	100 (27,000)	100 (55,000)	Total	100.0

Sources: Table: "Immigrant aliens or newcomers admitted to the United States for permanent residence, who gave Germany as their last permanent residence, years ended June 30, 1935, 1936, 1937, 1938, by sex, age, etc." YIVO, RG 278, Box 2, Folder 31 and Box 4; The Academic Assistance Council Annual Reports 1934, 1935, YIVO Archives; Fields (1938); Grebler (1976), LBIANY, ME 716, MM 29.

---

13 YIVO Archives, HIAS material, Table "Jewish Immigrant Aliens Admitted from July 1st 1933 to June 30, 1943." Because data were calculated on a fiscal-year basis, the dramatic rise in numbers (from Germany and Austria) is visible: 30,096 in fiscal year 1938/1939 and 19,880 in 1939/1940.
14 Davie and Koenig (1945), 11.

The great majority of the immigrants from Central Europe were Jews, and, therefore, social and demographic surveys relating to the immigrants generally apply to Jews specifically.

According to official immigration statistics, an unusually large proportion of the refugees had been engaged in their home countries in professional and commercial fields and in white-collar occupations, while the proportion of farmers, skilled and unskilled workers and servants was less than normal among former mass immigrations or refugees coming from other European and world countries.[15]

Table 17: Occupational structure of the immigrants to the U.S.A., 1933–1944

Field	Occupation	Number	Total in Field
Commerce and Industry			
	Merchants and Dealers	25,000	
	Agents	5,500	
	Manufacturers	1,800	32,300
Professions			
	Physicians	5,000	
	College Professors and School Teachers	3,500	
	Technical Engineers	2,500	
	Clergymen	2,400	
	Scientists and Literary people	1,900	
	Lawyers	1,800	16,100
The Arts			
	Musicians	1,200	
	Actors	800	
	Artists	700	2,700
Total			51,100

Source: Data cited by Davie and Koenig (1945), 12.

In the first period of immigration the professional composition of the immigrants was disproportionately weighted toward academics, artists and scientists. Special arrangements were often made to enable them to enter the country and to obtain employment at academic institutions or in consulting positions for the government or the industry.[16] Of about 2,000 university professors fleeing Central

---

15 Davie and Koenig (1945), 12.

16 Bentwich (1936); Report on the Work of the Jewish Refugee Committee from March, 1933 to January, 1935, WLL, CBF, MF 318/5, 123; also see various tables in YIVO Archives, RG 278, box 2, files 27, 31. See also Niederland (1988).

Europe, two thirds resettled in the United States.[17] This occupational structure later changed dramatically. In 1938, only 1,109, or about 6 percent, were professionals, academics or artists.[18]

Other features distinguishing the German immigrants in comparison with former immigrants were their educational background – most of them had gone beyond the elementary school level, and nearly a half had attended college or graduate school. They were primarily city people with a cosmopolitan outlook; many had travelled widely and knew languages other than their own. A good many of them were relatively well off. This of course, too, was particularly true of the refugees who arrived in the middle 1930s, when it was still possible to salvage a part of one's possessions, which was not the case with those who came from 1938 on.[19]

Britain

The Weimar Era

Britain had never experienced large-scale German-Jewish immigration before the 1930s. The German 19th century immigration into Britain was mainly of non-Jews, except for a number of famous scientists and industrial entrepreneurs, among them the founders of the British chemical and electric industrial concerns.[20] Moreover, after the end of WWI, Britain had declared its being a non-immigration country altogether.

The Nazi Era

In the early phase of the Jewish outflow from Nazi Germany Britain played a very minor role as a destination due to the British immigration policy, receiving only 4,000 German-Jews out of the total German-Jewish emigration of 93,000 in 1933–35, and reached a record of about 10,000 until 1938 (see Table 18).[21] The picture, however, changed significantly in 1938, following the *Anschluss* of Austria in March and the *Kristallnacht* pogrom in November of that year. New categories of entry permits were introduced, and on the basis of Jewish organizations' or

---

17 Krohn (1998).

18 YIVO Archives, RG 278, box 4; Fields (1938); Grebler (1976), LBIANY.

19 Davie and Koenig (1945), 12; Fields (1938), 30–31.

20 Holmes (1991); Loebl (1983); Travis (2004).

21 Traub (1936).

early immigrants' financial support and guarantees, the immigration officials were more flexible in granting entry permits.[22] The case of the Fraenkel family is illustrative: Eric Fraenkel immigrated in 1933 to become a student. In late 1938 he acted as guarantor for his sister's family who were transit migrants to the U.S. They came in December 1938 and proceeded with their journey after a month. His father, a successful textile importer-exporter, lost all his assets to the Nazis. Eric acted as guarantor for his parents, who arrived with no means in July 1939.[23]

Estimating the number of German Jews destined for Britain in those later years is rather complicated due to the high percentage of transit migrants who left Britain before or during WWII. This complication adds to the difficulties caused by the official statistics that do not distinguish between tourists and immigrants. In view of these constraints the following estimates seem to be the most reliable.

Table 18: The proportion of immigrants to Britain within the total Jewish emigration from Germany in selected periods

Period	Total From Germany (100%)	To Britain	
		Numbers	**Percentage of Total**
1933–1936	93,000	4,000	4.3
1933–1938	179,000	10,000*	10.0
1938–1941	170,000	35,000	20.6
1933–1941	270,000	45,000	16.7

* The British Prime Minister announced in Parliament on 21 November, 1938, that until then Britain absorbed 11,000 refugees, cited in Mock (1986), 96.
Sources: Traub (1936), covering January1933-June 1936, based on official German sources; AJR 6, June 1946; Rosenstock (1951, 1956); Strauss (1978), xx; Sherman (1973); Grenville (2002). There is not absolute consistency between the various sources in numbers and periods. Usually 1933–1938 applies to April 1933 through October 1938; 1933–1936 covers the first quarter of 1936; 1938–1939 = November 1938 through August 1939.

About 73,000 Jews seem to have arrived in Britain from Germany and Austria, and 10,000 from Czechoslovakia, between 1933 and 1941, making a total of 83,000 Jewish immigrants from Central Europe. The great majority of this movement took place after 1938, and included 9,000 to 10,000 Jewish children under the age of 18 who were brought to Britain with the *Kindertransport*.[24]

---

22 See Chapter 1, and in addition: Mock (1986), 96.
23 Interview with Eric Fraenkel, IWM Sound Archives, no. 16487.
24 Rosenstock (1951); Salomon Adler-Rudel, "Die juedischen Refugees in England (1943)," LBINY, Salomon Adler-Rudel Collection, AR 4473; Strickhausen (1998), 251–269.

As shown in Table 18, until 1938 Britain received only 10,000 German immigrants.[25] During the 18 months from the *Anschluss* of Austria in March 1938 to the outbreak of the war in September 1939, some 60,000 refugees came to Britain, half of them from Austria.[26] Austrian refugees made up more than a third of the total Central European immigrant population.[27] Of the immigrants from Germany, estimated to have totaled about 63,000 up to the war,[28] 45,000 were Jews, and the majority of them – about 35,000 – came between 1939 and 1941.[29]

Of all the Central Europeans who arrived and stayed in Britain until the war, about 20,000 re-emigrated during or after the war (13,000 to America, 1,200 to Palestine), and others – mainly non-Jewish political refugees – were repatriated.[30] It is estimated that about 50,000 of the total settled permanently in Britain.[31]

Demographic Profile of the Immigrants

Table 19 presents the age composition of the early immigrants from Germany, with its high percentage of people aged 20–40 in the prime of their careers. Compared to the age composition of German Jewry at the time, it reflects the selective character of the immigrants to Britain during the early 1930s, and may apply to German immigrants until 1938. However, while for the period 1933–1935 there are detailed statistics, the data are quite scarce for the mass immigration period of 1938/39. Moreover, the few data for the later period relate to all the refugees without distinguishing between Jewish and non-Jewish (political), German and Austrian, trans-migrants and immigrants. Therefore, regarding the age distribution over the entire period the estimation offered very carefully by S. Adler-Rudel is suggested, as follows:

Since the great majority came after 1938, it is reasonable that the age composition was largely affected by the high percentage of the *Kindertransport* children and of those who entered with special visas for over 60 years old granted by the government in late 1938. Thus, the overwhelming proportion of the later wave of mass refugee immigration over the early wave of selective immigration created the overall proportions of children and old people, untypical for an immigrant population.

---

25 Based on calculation of Home Office statistics cited by Sherman (1973); *Refugee Facts* (1939).
26 Grenville (2002).
27 Rosenstock (1951).
28 Calculation based on Home Office data cited by Sherman (1973).
29 Based on Grenville (2002).
30 AJR 6, June 1946
31 Berghahn (1984).

Table 19: Age distribution of German immigrants to Britain, 1933–1935

Age	Number	Percentage
0–19	588	14.5
20–40	2,592	63.9
40–49	543	13.4
50 +	314	7.7
Unknown	19	0.5
Total	4,055	100.0

Based on the data of the Jewish Refugee Committee Report on the Work 1933–1935, WLL, CBF, MF 318/5, 123.

Table 20: Age distribution of German immigrants to Britain, 1933–1939

Age	Number	Percentage
0–18	8,000	15.1
19–60	27,500	51.9
60+	17,500	33.0
Total	53,000	100.0

Based on Adler-Rudel "Die juedischen Refugees in England (1943)," LBIANY, Adler-Rudel Collection, AR 4473.

The occupational structure of the immigrants changed likewise in the post-1938 mass inflow. Statistics for 1933–1934 show that among 4,000 immigrants almost half were academics, free professions and students; more than a quarter were industrialists, technicians, engineers and artisans, and almost 20 percent were businesspeople (many of them with previous business connection in Britain), as shown in Table 21.

This composition was largely the outcome of the government policy to exempt scientists and industrialists from the implementation of the rigid Aliens Order, assuming that they could help in pulling the British economy out of its crisis.

Another interesting feature of the occupational structure is the tiny percentage of female immigrants who were formerly homemakers or without profession, which probably does not reflect the average rate within German Jewry at the time, and signifies the selective character of the early immigrants.

Table 21: Former professions of German immigrants to Britain, March 1933-October 1934

Occupation	Number	Of Which Women	Percentage	Percentage of Women
Students/pupils	836	348	20.7	
Academic Professions*	816	135	20.2	
Employers, Workers**	779	293	19.3	
Artists, Journalists	209	53	5.2	
Businesspeople	718	32	17.9	
Artisans	250	71	6.2	
Women's Professions***	138	138	3.4	
Without Profession	111	95	2.7	
Homemakers	178	178	4.4	
Total	4,035	1,343	100.0	33.3

* Probably including doctors and lawyers.
** Understood to be industrialists and technicians/skilled workers.
*** Mainly domestic workers and nurses.
Source: Jewish Refugee Committee Report on the Work 1933–1935, WLL, CBF, MF 318/5, 123.

The fact that there is not a separate category for free professions such as doctors and lawyers signifies the tiny number of those, who were unwelcome in Britain due to difficulties to adjust to the different health system and the objection of the relevant guilds. It should also be emphasized that the Jewish Refugee Committee's report is based on the card-index of those registered with the committee, and, as the following sample tells us, doctors came on the basis of direct personal connections and probably did not register with the committee.

The sample of individual cases discussed earlier as early immigrants from Germany[32] may illustrate also the typical profile of the those who arrived in England prior to 1938. Eric Fraenkel arrived in England to study medicine there on the expense of British businessmen who were in debt to his father.[33] Beatrice Musgrave's father, who arrived with his family in 1937, was a businessman who lived in Bradford before WWI, and had relatives in England.[34] Lotte Hamburger's father who immigrated in 1933 was a hat manufacturer who had largely exported to England.[35] Ellen Shiffman's father had medical contacts and was sponsored

---

32 See chapter 4.
33 Interview with Eric Fraenkel, IWM Sound Archives, no. 16487.
34 Refugee Voices, WLL, No. 86.
35 Personal interview, at the USHMM, Washington, D.C., 2005.

to come to England in 1937/8.[36] Edith Bülbring was a doctor and her connections enabled her to get a job and immigrate in 1933.[37] Hans Grünberg was in his practical training as a doctor and through personal connections got a research position in Cambridge.[38] Bernard Katz established contact with the physiologist Prof. Hill, one of the founders of the AAC, and arrived in 1935 with the help of relatives in England.[39] Ludwig Spiro studied machine engineering, and immigrated to Britain in 1936, before completing his diploma, because in Britain there was a great demand for engineers.[40] Liselotte Leschke left Germany for Britain in 1933 to study English.[41] Ingrid Heichelheim came to the Royal Academy of Music to study opera singing.[42] Max Milner enrolled in 1937 in Edinburgh University to study engineering.[43]

Contrary to the arrivals prior to 1938, those who reached Britain in the late 1930s and early 1940s held versatile occupations of all kinds.[44] Nevertheless, since the British policy in favor of industrialists, engineers and academics stayed valid throughout the 1930s, their proportions remained high.

In Conclusion: A Comparative Analysis

The above analyses indicate that the three groups under discussion varied in terms of demographic, occupational and economic composition as well as in the timing and dynamics of their migration. All of these factors were closely linked with each other. During the 1920s, both Palestine and the United States served as destinations for immigrating German Jews, while Britain experienced little German-Jewish immigration. The Jews immigrating to the United States were different from those who chose to go to Palestine. America attracted mainly young German-Jewish small or medium businessmen, while Palestine was the goal of young professionals and academics, mainly in the early stages of building their careers.

---

36 Refugee Voices No. 16.
37 IWM, no. 004532/02.
38 IWM, no. 004478.
39 IWM, no. 004508.
40 IWM, no. 004343.
41 Refugee Voices, WLL, No. 29.
42 Refugee Voices, WLL, No. 9.
43 Refugee Voices, WLL, No. 3.
44 Grenville (2002).

During the Nazi era, despite the common grounds for emigration, different groups of German Jews varied in the timing of their decision to emigrate, and accordingly their options to choose a destination changed. Those who made a quick decision to emigrate overseas for good were mainly young professionals whose prospects in Germany were dim. For the most part, they chose Palestine as their destination with the exception of high-ranking academics (both young and old) for whom special arrangements were made in both Britain and the United States, and those who had previous connections in these countries.

The great majority of German Jews who were driven to emigrate only after *Kristallnacht*, were typical refugees and reflected more or less the average profile of aging German Jews who had limited prospects for transferring what was left of their capital. These were accepted mainly in the U.S. and in Britain, since both nations responded to the events in Germany by loosening their rigid immigration regulations, whereas Palestine became increasingly closed, particularly following the Arab Revolt that broke out in 1936 and the Mandate White Paper of 1939 that severely restricted Jewish immigration.

The outcome of these developments was decisive in shaping the different profile of each immigrant group (Tables 22 and 23).

Table 22: Age distribution of the Jews in Germany and of Nazi era immigrants to Palestine, the U.S. and Britain (by percentage)

Age	Germany 1933	Palestine 1933–1938	U.S. 1934–1938	U.S. 1938–1941	Britain 1933–1939
0–20		29.0	30.0	18.0	15.1
0–24	28.2				
21–50		51.0	55.0	51.0	51.9
19–60					
25–60	55.4				
50/51+		12.0	15.0	31.0	
60+	16.3				33.0
Total	100.0	100.0	100.0 (27,000)	100.0 (55,000)	100.0 (53,000)

Source: Calculated on the basis of Tables 3, 11, 16, 19, above.

It may be difficult to define with any precision the profile of the immigrants to the U.S. and Britain. While the estimates for Germany and Palestine apply exclusively to Jews, those for the United States and Britain do not distinguish between Jews and non-Jews. Academics and artists who went to those countries included a significant number of non-Jewish political exiles. Our conclusions are therefore tentative. However, since many if not most immigrants from Germany were Jews or of Jewish descent, it is reasonable to apply the estimates in a broad sense to the Jews as a migrant and refugee population. The group who went to the U.S. was less homogeneous in terms of age, capital and skills. It included some stellar personalities and Nobel Prize laureates in the arts and sciences, though as time progressed, this influx was more middle- and lower-middleclass, representing the profile of German Jewry at large. The German Jews who immigrated to Britain came at about the same time as many Austrian and Czech Jews. Most of the immigrants came in the late 1930s, and with no possessions, though among them (as in the American case) was a small but visible group of artists and academics, many of them of Viennese origin, and – due to the British immigration policy – a considerable percentage of industrialists, engineers and technicians.

Table 23: Occupational structure of the Jews in Germany and of Nazi era immigrants to Palestine, the U.S. and Britain (by percentage)

Occupation	Germany 1933	Palestine 1933–1938	U.S. 1933–1945	Britain 1933–1934
Business	61.3	26.1	58.5	17.9
Professions/services	13.9	24.4	38.0	49.1
Industry	23.1	18.3	3.5	25.5
Agriculture	1.7	17.4		
Unknown/unskilled		13.8		7.2
Total	100.0	100.0	100.0	100.0

Source: Calculated on the basis of Tables 13, 14, 16, 17, 21, above.

To sum up, all three groups did not mirror the aging profile of German Jewry. However, the percentage of the working age and occupational character of the group who went to Palestine was more exceptional than the two other groups that mirrored more or less the profile of German Jewry.

Chapter 6
Towards Absorption of Mass Immigration from Germany: The Destination Perspective

The Advantage of Palestine

Jewish immigration to Palestine over hundreds of years was an act motivated mainly by a religious spiritual drive. From the last decades of the 19th century on, religious motivation was accompanied by a new national-Zionist ideological trend. On the eve of World War I, the Jewish community in Ottoman Palestine counted about 80,000, consisting of some 50,000 who belonged to the "Old *Yishuv*," those who settled out of religious motivation and for religious purposes in Palestine. They were joined by 30,000 who arrived in the recent three decades preceding the war as part of the mass migration from Eastern Europe for whom Palestine became a realistic possibility to build new life, and who were partly involved with the beginning of national-Zionist activity. A big step forward in combining Zionism with the Jewish immigration to Palestine was the creation of the Jewish National Home under the British Mandate in the post-WWI era, which allowed the World Zionist Organization to establish the Jewish Agency for Palestine and to be partly in charge of Jewish immigration and settlement. From then on Palestine began to attract more attention, Jewish immigration to Palestine soared and the Zionist machinery was involved in creating educational and preparatory training bases as well as in playing a significant role in the encounter with immigrants and organization of the Jewish community.

German Zionism

Examining German Zionism will allow us to understand the encounter between German-Jewish immigration and Palestine. German Zionism emerged during the latter part of the 19th century as a response to two interrelated processes – the mass appearance of Jewish immigrants from Eastern Europe – the *"Ostjuden"*– and the rise of modern anti-Semitism. Since the universities served as the meeting place of both, a whole range of responses developed among students regarding the "Jewish question," among them the Zionist response.

Note: This section is based primarily on Lavsky (1996).

DOI 10.1515/9783110501650-007

The German Zionist Federation (*Zionistische Vereinigung für Deutschland*, ZVfD) was a small organization, comprising three percent of German Jewry, and five percent of the World Zionist Organization (WZO). But inspite of its tiny dimensions it fulfilled a central role in founding the WZO in 1897 and in running it thereafter. During the ten years between the death of the movement founder, Theodor Herzl in 1904, up to World War I, German Zionism was the home of the Central Zionist Office, and German Zionists held key positions in the WZO. The "second generation" of German Zionists began already then to develop a radical version of Zionism, which called for Hebrew renaissance, personal devotion to the building of Palestine as the new homeland, and personal commitment to immigrate to Palestine. This revolutionary trend received a dramatic push during WWI, and was expressed during the Weimar period by the central role it took in promoting Palestine and the building of the national home on the German Zionist agenda. German Zionist leaders were key movers in the establishment of the *Keren Hayesod* (Jewish Foundation Fund, KH) in 1920, and they developed the unwritten covenant between the public-national capital and the Zionist Labor Movement during the 1920s.

Despite the fact that the Central Zionist Office moved in 1920 to London, and Eastern European Zionist leaders replaced the former German Zionist leaders, German Zionists continued to influence the economic sphere in shaping Zionist settlement policy and in filling key positions in all matters concerning the settlement project in Palestine. Arthur Ruppin was the head of the Zionist Settlement Department from 1920 on. Arthur Hantke was director of KH from 1926, Felix Rosenblüth was the head of the Zionist Organization Department in 1925, Georg Landauer the head of the JA Immigration Department in the 1920s, and Julius Berger the director of JNF in Palestine.

German Zionism therefore paved the way and shaped the character of German immigration to Palestine during the 1920s, and became the bridge on which the mass immigration of the Nazi era could move. The role of German Zionism would thus be decisive also in shaping the patterns of the German-Jewish identity and integration in Palestine.

German-Jewish Palestinian Community on the Eve of the Nazi Era

The tiny number of 3,300 immigrants from Germany during the 1920s joined the group of German Zionists who came already prior to WWI and had an enormous impact on the development of the Jewish community in Palestine. Among these veterans were the brothers Oskar, Alfred and Joseph Treidel, engineers and industrial entrepreneurs; Arthur Biram who founded and directed the famous Reali

High School in Haifa; the founder of the Palestine Office Arthur Ruppin; the leading agronomists Selig Soskin and Wilhelm Brünn (who was also a physician), and doctor Elias Auerbach.[1]

These pioneers were joined during the 1920s by groups of young people trained in agriculture or industrial and building works, among them the *Avoda*, *Zvi* and *Markenhof* groups who joined the *kibbutzim* founded in the early 1920s such as Ein Harod, and founded Kibbutz Bet Zera, and the *Blau-Weiss* workshops group for building industries. Many other immigrants came as Zionist functionaries, on the invitation of various institutions or on their own initiative. Arthur Hantke, Georg Landauer, Julius Berger, Felix Rosenblüth – all of whom have already been mentioned – came in the early 1920s, and Ruppin returned to Palestine in 1920. They were joined by many others, among them a substantial number of architects, engineers and academics who took central, even leading, part in designing and laying foundations for the Zionist settlement project: The architect Alex Baerwald, who had already designed the Technion building – the Institute for Technical Education in Haifa (later: Israel Institute of Technology) – before the war, settled in Haifa in 1925. The architect Richard Kaufmann was invited by Ruppin in 1920 to head the planning office of the Palestine Office and the adjacent Palestine Land Development Company (PLDC). He was the first architect to introduce settlement planning as a discipline and modern architecture to Palestine as a style. He designed the first *Moshav Ovdim* (labor cooperative agricultural settlement) Nahalal in the Yezre'el Valley, which served as the model for many *moshavim*.[2] His assistant Charlotte (Lotte) Cohn joined him in 1921.[3] The architect Fritz Kornberg designed the Hebrew University's open theater on Mount Scopus; the engineer Martin Goldschmidt together with the geologists Stephan Löwengardt and Leo Picard laid the basis for the irrigation system;[4] and the scholars Gerhard Gershom Scholem, David Zvi (Hartwig) Baneth, Shlomo Dov Goitein, Ernst Akiva Simon and Shmuel Samburski were among the leading figures in the Hebrew University of Jerusalem founded 1925. Other leading figures and pioneers were David Werner Senator, the chief administrator of the Hebrew University;[5] Walter Moses, industrial pioneer; leading lawyers such as Moshe Zmoira; pioneer physicians such as Felix Danziger and Arieh Ulitzki; the gymnastics and sport educator Ernst

---

1 Lichtheim records names and positions of 27 Zionists who settled in Palestine before the war, see: Lichtheim (1951).
2 Warhaftig (2007).
3 Sonder (2006), see Chapter 4.
4 Gross (1999).
5 *Toldot Ha'Universita* (1997–2013).

Emmanuel Simon; the gardeners Haim Latte and Eliezer Burchardt; the librarian Karola Lorch; the journalist Gerda Arlosoroff (Luft) and many others.[6]

This small but highly select and visible group of able and dedicated individuals marked the presence of German Jews in Palestine in the 1920s. Later in the decade, though, Palestine's Jewish economy faced a deep recession concurrently with the deflationary years in Germany, and attracted neither Zionist nor non-Zionist German Jews. However, those immigrants of the 1920s would later be instrumental in shaping the patterns of organization, absorption, and integration of the large influx of immigrants from Nazi Germany.

The World Jewish Organizations in the Service of German-Jewish Immigration to Palestine

The wave of Jewish immigration from Nazi Germany came during a crucial time period in the not yet mature Jewish economy. The trial and error phase of the 1920s had laid the basis for the expansion and development of a modern economy.

During the first half of the 1930s, against the background of the world economic crisis, Palestine enjoyed a time of prosperity. The High Commissioner of Palestine, Sir Arthur Wauchope, responded to the prosperity and to the anticipation of continuing inflow of Jewish capital by enlarging the quotas for immigrants. In addition, the government issued special certificates for Youth *Aliya*, allowing the entrance of about 700 youngsters aged 15–17 from Germany during 1933–1935.[7] Palestine thus took the largest portion of Jewish international migration, including around 33,000 German-Jewish immigrants.

The international Jewish response to the establishment of the Nazi regime in Germany focused on Palestine as a safe haven for persecuted Jews. The prosperity in Palestine enabled the Zionist authorities to initiate the Transfer Agreement of 1933 with the Nazi government, and encouraged the Central British Fund (CBF), established in 1933 by British Jewry, to support German-Jewish emigration and resettlement to put Palestine on the top of its agenda, and laid the basis for a special Zionist settlement apparatus aimed specifically for German Jews in Palestine.[8]

---

6 Lavsky (1996), 103; Rothschild (1972), Chapter 3; interviews conducted by the author in 1982 with Mali Danziger, Meta and Meir Pflanter, Paul Jacobi, Haim Latte, Karola Lorch, Shmuel Samburski, Emmanuel Ernst Simon, Akiva Ernst Simon, and Arieh Ulitzki, OHD, Project no. 183.
7 Bentwich (1936).
8 Annual Report of the Council for German Jewry (1936), WLL; Gelber (1990), Chapter 1; Fraenkel (1994), Chapter 1; Lavsky (1996), 227–253; and see Chapter 4, above.

Although Palestine ceased to be a preferred destination over the second half of the 1930s due to economic and political crises and the change in the British Mandate immigration policy, the stream of immigrants from Germany did not subside, except for the year 1937, and during the four years 1936–1939, Palestine absorbed 27,300 more immigrants from Germany, due to the preferential treatment of the Mandatory policy towards immigration from Germany.

A Machinery of Absorption

A considerable part of the immigration from Germany to Palestine was an organized enterprise based on planning and advocating settlement projects, creating a wide system of information, and providing facilities for preparation in Germany. Many immigrants could thus arrive organized by the Jewish Agency and others were assisted by an elaborate and efficient settlement apparatus working with the JA, and run by their compatriots, and for which the early immigrants of the 1920s were of utmost importance. Thus, in a sense, the concept of chain migration is applicable to the immigration to Palestine, not just in relation to individual immigration assisting pattern, but as a concept referring to the entire immigration move from Germany to Palestine.

The positive economic development in Palestine in the beginning of the 1930s was accompanied by the consolidation of the Jewish Agency as the leader in immigration and settlement, together with the strengthening of the Jewish National Council as the authority responsible for the wellbeing of the *Yishuv*. These two bodies were now able to respond to the challenge posed by the human and economic quality of the immigrants from Germany; they created new machinery, devoted exclusively to their absorption and settlement, run almost entirely by German Zionists, in Palestine and abroad. The early German immigrants in Palestine founded in 1932 the *Hitahdut Olei Germanya* (Association of Immigrants from Germany, HOG). With the arrival of the Austrian refugees in 1938–9 it changed its name to *Hitahdut Olei Germanya ve'Ostriya*), which saw its main purpose in designing an elaborate network for absorbing the newcomers into the Jewish economic, social and cultural system.[9] Established in 1933, the network included the CBF in Britain, the National Council in Palestine, the German members of the JA Executive, and the HOG. Following the 18th Zionist Congress in Prague in August 1933 a triple branched organization was established, including the Central Bureau

---

9 Lavsky (2003); Mathias Marburg, *HOG und Landsmanschaften* (seminar paper, in possession of the author).

for the Settlement of German Jews in Palestine, based in London and headed by Chaim Weizmann (who at that time was out of office as the President of the WZO), the German Department of the JA in Jerusalem headed by Arthur Ruppin, and the HOG, represented by Georg Landauer and Werner Senator. German-Jewish immigrants thus benefited from an extra assistance system run by their compatriots. The HOG became the agency mediating between the authorities and the immigrants.

The new system designed the integration and settlement process on the basis of Zionist guidelines accompanied by new standards and new patterns and dimensions in immigration absorption. First of all, it benefited from the new input of professionals – business and finance experts, people with strong backgrounds of social work, trained physicians, many of them German-Jewish veterans already integrated in the country and its leadership.

The HOG's activity was in a variety of spheres – economic, cultural and social – especially for those who were not taken care of by the *Histadrut* – the General Labor Union.[10] The first area of its activity was economic assistance. HOG added immigrant houses as first shelter, in addition to those supported by the JA; special labor bureaus (which acted in cooperation with the *Histadrut*); advising in legal and economic matters; and agricultural training. But more important and innovative for the *Yishuv* were its activities designed for economic absorption in the long run. The HOG established a loan fund – financed by its members and with the help of the German Department of the JA – for independent urban and rural workers and businesses. A second innovation was the enterprise for vocational adjustment, which helped immigrants to adopt new trades fit for the demand in the Palestine economy.

The second realm of HOG activity was social welfare. The National Council had already established a Welfare Department by the beginning of the 1930s, but this department did not act in the field of immigrants' absorption. Among the veteran German immigrants there were a number of modern professional social workers who worked out a full system to treat newcomers, which acted through the National Council's department and its welfare bureaus adjacent to municipal authorities. The range of activities designed for the newcomers included provisions to help with sustenance, accommodation, healthcare, child care, education, vocational training, homes for the elderly and children's homes. Some of them, like the *Ahava* Children's Home, were transferred from Germany.

---

10 For details and archival sources of the following, consult Lavsky (2003).

Figure 12: Children of *Ahava* Children's Home after moving from Berlin to Haifa in 1933, in Hebrew class. Courtesy of the Central Zionist Archives.

Actually social work was by and large connected with the economic activity designed for the long run: establishing small farms and workshops in the colonies for workers to increase their income; child care to allow mothers to integrate into the labor market; and financial provisions for settlement and educational institutions earmarked to train newcomers from Germany and help them adjust.

A third and not less important area of HOG activity was in the cultural sphere. The HOG designed programs directed to the integration of the immigrants into the Hebrew national culture, and to make use of the cultural assets imported by them as inputs for developing new cultural standards: Hebrew courses, lecture series, assisting academics – teachers and students – to integrate into academic teaching, art and research institutions; and supporting immigrants' new initiatives such as the establishment of innovative schools. This kind of initial support for education was also guided, like the social work, by the idea of constructive support. For example, there was assistance to educational institutions to help them in absorbing many new students, which meant also an increase of the demand for teachers that could be met by the new supply of teachers, who were assisted by the HOG in adjusting to the Hebrew educational system.

The HOG also worked in cooperation with the cultural department of the *Histadrut* headed by Jacob Sandbank, himself a German immigrant, and assisted a variety of German-Jewish religious associations and congregations. The CBF financed the training of many more. The beneficiaries of the CBF support included the Youth *Aliya*, the Bezalel crafts academy for the development of new branches in metalwork and lithography, and the enlargement of the Ben Shemen Youth Village (whose founding director was the German Zionist Siegfried Lehmann), as well as the transfer of the *Ahava* Children's Home from Berlin to Haifa and then to Kfar Bialik.[11]

American Infrastructure

German Jews in the U.S.A.

German-Jewish American Diaspora was created during the 19th century, as a part of a huge emigration stream from Germany to the U.S.A. The estimate is that by 1914 some 250,000 American Jews came from German speaking countries, of whom the greater part came from Germany alone. Before the mass migration from Eastern Europe, which started in the early 1880s, German Jews constituted to a large degree the entire American Jewish community.[12] By that time, second and third generation offspring of these Jews had established themselves in the upper social and economic echelon, and quite a few of them had become bankers, industrialists, prominent lawyers, and large-scale entrepreneurs, such as Louis D. Brandeis, Felix Frankfurter, Louis Marshall, Julius Rosenwald, Jacob Schiff, and Felix M. Warburg. About 97 percent of all the garment industry in New York was owned by German Jews.[13] As a consequence, the American Jewish community system and all its organizations and representative leadership were composed of Jews of German origin. As part of their communal responsibility, they developed a kind of absorption machinery, which typically aimed at dispersing the millions of new immigrants and at forming the Eastern European Jews in their own image. However, with the increasing flood of immigration, the Americanized German Jews gradually represented a minority – though still powerful – as opposed to the growing Eastern European majority. The two communities were in conflict and separate from each other to a large extent. They made their homes in separate

---

11 Bentwich (1936), 130ff.
12 Barkai (1994), 9.
13 Barkai (1994), 207.

quarters in New York or Chicago, each preserving its own long-lasting social and cultural milieu. The division thus became a persisting characteristic of American Jewish community before WWI.[14]

Immigrants from Germany during the 1920s

As already noted in Chapter 3, the unstable German post-WWI economy pushed many Germans to emigrate. Immigrants to the United States came mainly from the ranks of business people and, in particular, members of the younger generation who saw no future for themselves in Germany.

The American Jewish community at this time numbered approximately 4 million; during the 1920s, it absorbed 360,000 additional Jewish immigrants (see Table 1, above). Among them were some 7,300 German Jews, whose arrival peaked at almost 2,000 entries in 1923–1924.[15] The newcomers were concentrated mainly in New York City and were quite different from the German Jews who had come to the United States in the 19th century, some of whom had experienced a dynamic rise into the upper middle class.[16] The new immigrants of the 1920s belonged mostly to the young generation who immigrated in order to support their impoverished families they left behind. They encountered a different America and experienced significant occupational and economic obstacles. Most of them arrived without any previous academic training, and lacked the capital and the language skills needed to open businesses, and they integrated initially into low-level labor. However, following the initial period of hard labor, training and studies they eventually pursued successful professional careers, notably in medicine, while others found their opportunity in such fields as communication and the arts, and in the metal and chemical industries. The women immigrants integrated mainly in housekeeping occupations and did not manage to climb up the occupational ladder.[17] Overall, however, the impact of this migration on the occupational and economic profile of American Jews was muted.

---

14 Barkai (1994), 210.
15 Bickelmann (1980), Table 6 on p. 146; Dr. Harry S. Linfield, the Director of the Jewish Statistical Bureau in New York, cites the number of 6,670 Jewish immigrants from Germany, between 1920–1929: Linfield (1933), Table 3, 41–42. Max Malina, who was the founder of the German-Jewish Center that welcomed and assisted German-Jewish immigrants, estimates their number at 25–30,000 German Jewish immigrants, including all German-speaking Jewish immigrants between 1918 and 1931. See: Malina (1931), 16.
16 Barkai (1994); Diner (1992).
17 Malina (1931), 23–26.

German-Jewish immigrants in the post-World War I period were quite active in constructing aid organizations for the newcomers, thereby laying the infrastructure for the later arrivals of the 1930s. Among these, the most important were the Prospect Unity Club (1923), the Deutsch-jüdischer Club (German-Jewish Club), 1924 and, in 1926, the German-Jewish Center in New York that concentrated primarily on assisting young newcomers.[18]

All-American Absorption Machinery

America was, after all, a classic immigration country. Moreover, its already existing Jewish community was quite well organized to welcome the newcomers.[19] On the other hand, against the economic crisis and the unusual socio-economic profile of the new immigrants, there was a great fear of increasing unemployment, particularly in the professions and white collar branches.

As a result, it was the first time in its history as an immigrant absorbing country that the United States established absorption mechanisms under government auspices. In 1933, the U.S. participated in creating the Intergovernmental High Commission for Refugees Coming from Germany. The first effort to provide for coordination of organizations assisting refugees coming from Germany was the Joint Clearing Bureau set up by the American Jewish Joint Distribution Committee (JDC). The work of the Clearing Bureau was limited to referring requests for information or help to appropriate organizations, such as the National Council of Jewish Women, the Hebrew Sheltering and Immigrant Aid Society (HIAS), and the various emergency committees that had formed to aid physicians, scholars and musicians. In 1934 the JDC led efforts to establish a separate agency that could coordinate refugee aid work in a more comprehensive way. The idea for such an organization took concrete shape in March 1934 when leaders of 18 American organizations concerned with helping refugees from Germany held a meeting with James G. McDonald, the League of Nations High Commissioner for Refugees Coming from Germany.

The National Coordinating Committee for Aid to Refugees and Emigrants Coming from Germany (National Coordinating Committee, NCC), was established in June the same year. Joseph P. Chamberlain was chair of the new organization, Paul F. Warburg, treasurer, and Cecilia Razovsky, executive director and secretary. Financed through Jewish fundraising organizations, the NCC coordinated the refugee aid work of approximately 20 refugee and social welfare organizations,

---

18 Malina (1931), 23–26. Malina devotes most of his account to the various organizations.
19 Laqueur (2001), 129–134.

including both Jewish and non-Jewish groups. It also acted as an information center for refugee issues, conveyed the views of the member agencies on immigration to the government in Washington, D.C., and to a small extent administered direct relief to refugees upon arrival.

Over time the NCC also laid the groundwork to enable refugees arriving in New York to resettle in communities elsewhere in the United States. By August 1936 local committees to assist refugees had been established in ten major cities. The local committees would seek out employment opportunities for refugees and help them establish their new lives. Ultimately the NCC developed a network of nearly 500 participating committees.

In the spring of 1938, President Franklin D. Roosevelt established the President's Advisory Committee on Political Refugees, under the chairmanship of James G. McDonald, to serve as a liaison between private American agencies and the Intergovernmental Committee on Refugees that was created at the Evian Conference in July 1938. He was nominated Honorary Chairman of the National Coordinating Committee, and another member of the Governing Body of the High Commission was the Chairman Joseph Perkins Chamberlain,

In the same year the NCC established the National Coordinating Committee Fund to seek broader national support for the program and to provide financing for the NCC as well as some of the cooperating agencies. The organizations besides the NCC that received subventions through the fund included the Greater New York Coordinating Committee, which coordinated the work of refugee aid organizations in New York and also worked directly with refugees through its various departments (Employment, Self-Support, Social and Cultural Adjustment of Newcomers, and Retraining and Resettlement of Foreign Physicians); the Jewish Social Service Association (German Department); the Jewish Family Welfare Society of Brooklyn; the National Council of Jewish Women (New York and Brooklyn Sections); the Emergency Committee in Aid of Displaced Foreign Scholars; and Trade Winds, Inc., Exchange Shop.

In May 1939 Harry Greenstein of the Associated Jewish Charities, Baltimore, was brought in to conduct an assessment of the NCC's operations. The central conclusion of his report was that due to the increased flow of refugees arriving, the NCC had outgrown its original design. He called for a thorough reorganization, and the formation of a new organization that would have a full range of operational departments in order to centralize the administration of services and relief to refugees upon arrival. Incorporated on 15 May and beginning operations in June 1939, the National Refugee Service (NRS) took over the work of the NCC, the NCC Fund, and the Greater New York Coordinating Committee. The NRS effectively consolidated and expanded refugee services along the lines proposed by Greenstein in his report. Although the NRS was formally nonsectarian, it had a more specifically Jewish identity than the NCC. Its board of directors was almost entirely Jewish, and its work focused on Jewish refugees. NRS became the most active body combining all groups working to aid German refugees.[20]

The British Government, the British Jews, and the Refugees

Until 1938, the British government held to its rigid immigration policy, exempting only academics, industrialists, engineers and technicians from the implementation of the Aliens Order, provided they had already a work place or financial guarantees. This policy was based on the demand of the worsening local economy that was much in need of these kinds of professions, and was supported by civil, Jewish and non-Jewish organizations. In May 1933, Sir William Henry Beveridge, the Director of the London School of Economics and Political Science, founded the Academic Assistance Council, with Lord Rutherford as the President. It was assisted financially by the Central British Fund for German Jewry (CBF) founded in 1933 that financed fellowships, institutions, laboratories and industrial projects for absorbing German-Jewish academics. The Joint Foreign Committee of the two main organizations of British Jews – the Board of Deputies of British Jews, and the Anglo-Jewish Association – established the Jewish Academic Committee on behalf of German-Jewish scholars in the field of Jewish Studies. Within three years more than 200 academics found places.[21]

British Jews were quite quick to establish a whole network of organizations to assist immigration and absorption of German Jews. The first organizational aid initiative was undertaken by a German Jew, Otto M. Schiff (nephew of Jacob Schiff, a prominent person in American Jewry), the president of the Jews' Temporary Shelter, who founded the Jewish Refugee Committee as a roof organization of all Jewish aid societies, with its seat in London, first in Woburn House and later in Bloomsbury House, together with non-Jewish refugee aid organizations.[22] Another organization, the Council for German Jewry, was founded in 1936, aiming to collaborate with American Jews, but in 1939 the cooperation broke down and

---

20 Guide to the Records of the National Refugee Service 1934–1952 (bulk 1939–1946) YIVO Archives, RG 248 (http://findingaids.cjh.org/?pID=1865416, accessed 29 May, 2016); Guide to the papers of Joseph Perkins Chamberlain (1873–1951), 1933–1951, YIVO Archives, RG 278; Breitman et al. (2009), 2–3; Hirshler(1955), 89–100; Fields (1938), 131–133; White (1957).
21 Zahl-Gottlieb (1998), 41–46.
22 Stent (1991); Strickhausen (1998).

it changed its name to Council for Jewish Refugees. The Central British Fund, founded in 1933, was not meant specifically for immigrants to Britain. On the contrary, its chief target was to solve the German-Jewish problem through immigration and settlement in Palestine.

These organizations were instrumental in supporting the entrance and the economic absorption of refugees by guaranteeing their financial support in order to counter the harsh government orders, particularly after 1938. Among the projects of the post-1938 era initiated and supported particularly by Jewish organizations was the *Kindertransport* to rescue children, run by the Children's Inter-Aid Committee, formed in 1936, which merged in March 1939 with the Movement for the Care of Children, to become the Refugee Children's Movement. It was assisted by other organizations, such as B'nai B'rith, WIZO (Women's International Zionist Organization), and the Youth *Aliya*, which took children into its training camps. The government was willing to admit 10,000 children up to the age of eighteen, on a temporary basis, provided their maintenance was guaranteed and they were prepared for eventual onward migration once their training had been completed or they reached the age of eighteen, whichever came first. The number of unaccompanied children who thus reached English shores amounted to almost 11,000, of whom 9,354 were brought over by the Refugee Children's Movement, 431 by the Children's Inter-Aid Committee, and 1,850 by the Youth *Aliya*. The great majority were Jewish, from Germany, Austria and Czechoslovakia, most of them between December 1938 and September 1939. These children and youth were put in foster homes or hostels in London and other major cities. Other children came with Jewish schools set up earlier in Germany, and transferred to Britain.[23]

Another emergency project initiated by the Jewish organizations as a result of pressure from the *Reichsvertretung der Juden in Deutschland* (formerly the *Reichsvertretung der deutschen Juden*) to rescue threatened Jews from Germany and Austria brought about an additional government concession, to admit a group of refugees aged 18–30, under the same provision that this rescue operation was to be of a temporary nature. An old army transit camp in Richborough, Kent, named after Lord Kitchener, a site derelict since World War I, was put at the disposal of the Jewish Refugee Committee. The camp began receiving refugees in February 1939 and ended with the outbreak of war in September, after which most of the residents chose to enlist in the British army. By that time it housed 3,200 young men, mainly newly trained craftsmen. Where the residents had wives and children they were lodged nearby. Three young English Jews, Jonas and Phineas May

---

23 Laqueur (2001); Stent (1991); Strickhausen (1998).

and M. Banks, who were later to become commissioned officers in the Pioneer Corps, were put in charge of the management of the camp.[24]

Figure 13: A Jewish youth, wearing a numbered tag, sits on a staircase with her head in her hands after her arrival in England with the *Kindertransport*, December 1938. Courtesy of the U.S. Holocaust Memorial Museum.

There were two additional initiatives that originated with the government, based on demands of the British market. One was the project of supporting the founding of new industries in the crisis bitten North-Eastern regions. This project was

---

24 WLL, title page of the Kitchener Camp, Richborough, Kent Records, 1939–1988; Tydor Baumel (1981); Stent (1991).

combined with new regulations that facilitated the entry of refugee industrialists.[25] The second was the great demand for domestic servants that was implemented in the issuing of domestic visas for refugee women.[26]

Figure 14: Group portrait of girls from the 5th Avenue Hostel who came to England on a *Kindertransport.* 1943. Courtesy of the U.S. Holocaust Memorial Museum.

---

25 Loebl (1983, 1991).
26 Kushner (1991).

Figure 15: Group portrait of Jewish refugees in the Kitchener refugee camp, June 1939. Courtesy of the U.S. Holocaust Memorial Museum.

In Conclusion

While in all three destinations the challenge of German-Jewish mass immigration was met with unprecedented organizational efforts by both governmental and civil Jewish authorities, there were immense differences between them. It seems that Palestine had the greatest advantage above other destinations caused by a number of factors: the permissive governmental policy during the initial stage of German-Jewish immigration, based on the prospect of potential German-Jewish economic contribution to the country's absorptive capacity; the inherent interest of the Jewish national home to grow and absorb immigration combined with the special privilege of the Jewish national home as a kind of autonomy; and the infrastructure laid by German Zionism as a bridge between Germany and Palestine. All these factors resulted in creating absorption machinery, a new phenomenon in the history of the *Yishuv*, and with no parallel in other immigration countries at the time. In many ways it was a harbinger and a model for modern immigration absorption policy that works via the *Landsmannschaft* organization to facilitate and smooth the integration process. However, even in this sphere it was unique, since the people in charge at the top of the hierarchy – the relevant JA departments – to the bottom – the secondary agents of the JA, were all members of the *Landsmannschaft*. This machinery worked even when political and economic circumstances deteriorated in the later phase of the 1930s, thus enabling the continuance of the process of settlement and absorption.

In both the U.S.A. and the U.K., the infrastructure for encountering and absorbing German-Jewish mass immigration was created as an emergency system against the backdrop of anti-immigration policy and public non-Jewish reluctance, based on the economic situation. By then, however, in both countries veteran Jewish welfare organizations joined hands with non-Jewish organizations and the government to create an absorption system, unprecedented in both. While in the U.S. this activity was targeted towards facilitating absorption while avoiding harm to the American economy, in Britain the main goal was to enable the very initial steps – permission to enter on the basis of emergency work permits. Thus, while in the U.S.A. the new system was shaped to meet a long-term absorption challenge, in Britain it was an emergency system for refugees.

The differences in the attitudes and systems developed in the destination countries to encounter the immigrants were decisive factors in the process of adjustment and settlements of the immigrants, as will be discussed in the following chapters.

Chapter 7
The Encounter and Integration in Palestine

Economic Aspects

The wave of Jewish immigration from Nazi Germany came during a crucial time period in the not yet mature Jewish economy in Palestine. The trial and error phase of the 1920s laid the basis for the expansion and development of a modern economy. The German immigrants constituted a significant part in the new wave of mass immigration (the 5th *Aliya*) that brought into the country in the years 1932-1935 161,000 immigrants and 86,000 more in the crisis years 1936–1939, as seen in Table 24. German Jews immigrating to Palestine during the prosperous years comprised about 15 percent of the total immigration. In the following years 1936–1939, however, against the background of recession, political violence and restrictions posed by the government their proportion grew. They counted now almost 32 percent of the total of 86,000 immigrants. This growing percentage reflects the Mandate immigration policy of reducing the number of immigration certificates from 1936 on, but still giving priority to German applicants.[1] Thus, within the entire 5th *Aliya* of 247,000 immigrants in the years 1932–1939 the proportion of the German immigrants was 21.3 percent.

Table 24: Proportion of immigrants from Germany in the 5th *Aliya*, 1932–1939

Period*	Total 5th *Aliya*	Immigrants from Germany	% of Immigrants from Germany in Total
1932–1935	161,000	24,850**	15.4
1936–1939	86,000	27,300	31.7
1932–1939	247,000	52,500	21.3

* Periods dictated by the changes in the status of Palestine as a destination. Based on Tables 1 and 7 above.
** including 350 immigrants of the year 1932, Niederland (1996), 26 and Table 6, above.

The young Jewish economy was just ripe to respond favorably to the challenge of expanding supply and demand forces of the immigrants, and to absorb new capital investments. The German proportion in the growing supply and demand forces was decisive, as can be viewed in Table 25, regarding their part in capital

---

1 Halamish (2006), 302.

DOI 10.1515/9783110501650-008

import. Although the only existing data relate to the number of immigrants who came as "capitalists" and there are few data relating to the amount of their individually imported capital, it is clear that the proportion of capitalists within the total of German immigrants reached almost 40 percent and that German capitalists constituted about a third of the total number of capitalist immigrants from all countries, relatively much more than the proportion of all German immigrants in the entire 5th *Aliya*. It may be concluded, therefore, that the role of the German immigrants in the growing supply and demand forces was decisive.

Table 25: Capitalists in the 5th *Aliya*

	Number	% in Total	% in Capitalist	% in German Aliya
Total Aliya	247,000	100		
Capitalist	64,200	26		
German Aliya	52,500	21		
German Capitalists	19,900	8	31	38

Calculation based on Metzer (1998) and Gelber (1990).

Those who came during the first wave of 1933–1935 could bring with them a considerable part of their capital, and others could make use of their skills and professions, for which there was demand in Palestine, and the economic impact of the immigrants was recognized and appreciated.[2]

Thus, the composition of motives and the socio-demographic profile of the immigrants from Germany to Palestine combined with the economic situation in Palestine were crucial in shaping the economic absorption and role of the new immigrants. However, there was another contributing factor in the process of absorption, namely the economic culture of the immigrants.

The Economic Role in the Palestine Economy

The German-Jewish input in the sphere of production, marketing and consumption patterns might be considered especially significant for Palestine, whose business culture was shaped by the Eastern European legacy, on the one hand, and by the Oriental environment, on the other. In all the branches of economy the German

---

2 Gelber (1990); Getter (1979); Miron (2005); Niederland (1983).

input was a combination of new demand – posed by the wave of Central European immigrants, and new supply of modern technology and professional experience, accompanied by capital import in the form of machinery and equipment from Germany in the framework of the Transfer Agreement with Nazi Germany.

The proportion of industrialists and engineers within the immigrating group to Palestine was high. They introduced new branches into industry, in particular pharmacology and medical equipment, and cleaning materials and services. They shaped the infant Palestinian-Jewish industry in scope, quality, diversity and design, as illustrated by gourmet food production such as sausage, fine chocolate and cheese, and by furniture production, associated with the names of Strauss (dairy) and Zoglobeck (sausage), Oppenheimer (chocolate) and Wissmann (furniture). The input of German immigrants was felt also in other branches, such as metal and electricity.[3]

The German immigrants – as customers and as entrepreneurs – particularly refashioned the realm of commerce in European style hitherto unknown in Palestine. They introduced chain marketing, department stores, delicatessen shops, specialized high fashion textiles, clothing, dress, shoes and accessories stores, and more. All these engaged artistically designed show windows, products and packing. Their impact was felt even in food marketing. There was indeed no resemblance between the old groceries and the new ones in terms of aesthetics and hygiene, politeness and good order.[4]

Another imprint of the newcomers was felt in the field of tourism, vacation and catering services. They introduced the type of family guesthouse (*Pension*) and restaurants (*Mittagstisch*) run by women for regular customers and for vacationers and European-style coffee houses. They also integrated into the expanding finance services with many new private family banks.

The input of the German immigrants in the field of agriculture was not less significant. The proportion of agriculture in Jewish Palestine was unique among Jewish communities. Immigration to Palestine was involved in vocational training, and the immigration, and the absorption system established by the Jewish Agency particularly encouraged agricultural training. Therefore, among German Jews immigrating to Palestine, the proportion of those defining themselves as agricultural laborers or farmers was considerable. This means that they decisively linked immigration with prior acquisition of new vocations.

Jewish agricultural development in Palestine reached a certain stage of maturity by the beginning of the 1930s. The hitherto division between the private sector's plantations and the public sector's mixed agriculture gave way to a newly expanding variety of mixed agriculture based on cooperation between the two

---

3 For a detailed survey see Gelber (1990), 398–414.
4 Gelber (1990), 414–419.

sectors. This development enabled the immigrants to implement new types of farming for which German entrepreneurship was highly appropriate. About a quarter of the German immigrants integrated into the agricultural sector and established new settlements, among them 14 *kibbutzim* such as Giv'at Brenner, Hazore'a, Ein Gev and Dorot, the cooperative villages Ramot Hashavim and Kfar Yedidya, the village Kfar Shemaryahu, the colony Nahariya, and more.

Figure 16: Kibbutz Hazore'a just established by immigrants from Germany, September 1938. Courtesy of the Central Zionist Archives.

They introduced new marketing branches, such as egg production and beekeeping for honey. They also innovated forms of settlement based on combining private enterprise with some degree of cooperative production and marketing and changed standards of work and production.[5]

The economic contribution and the general success of economic integration should not hide the problems and failures of those many professionals and intellectuals who could not find employment and had to make radical changes in their careers and sacrificed a lot. Marianne Veith, who immigrated with her fiancée Martin Einstein in early 1935 and was among the first capitalist settlers in the colony Benyamina, described retrospectively the poor living conditions, the lack of essential

---

5 Beling (1967), 75–125; Oren (1989).

facilities such as electricity, local medical aid, and transportation, which caused the loss of her child. The couple's hard work for many years to come had a deleterious affect on her husband's health in the long run. Another couple, Martin and Edith Münzeshimer, arrived in Palestine in 1936, and although they wanted to settle down as farmers, they had to put up with being construction workers, he for 23 years, and she – for 6 years.[6] Wolf Alexander, a specialist in German literature, became a bookkeeper in a travel agency and lost his academic career.[7] Not all the immigrants adjusted successfully, and there were those who felt neglected, who tried and did not manage economically and who left the country to try their fortune elsewhere. This was particularly true during the economic crisis of the second half of the 1930s.[8] Kurt Beer, a lawyer from Berlin, who came in 1933 and underwent occupational change, did not manage to find employment and in desperation went to Prague.[9]

Figure 17: Women settlers of Ramot Hashavim sitting in front of the newly built chicken coop, 1933. Courtesy of the Central Zionist Archives.

---

6 Retrospective interviews, cited in Römer (1987), 157–162, 205–208.

7 Private communication.

8 As exemplified in letters of complaint and requests for support by German immigrants to the German Department within the Jewish Agency in the 1930s. See Rautenberg-Alianov (2013), Personal Collection.

9 His letter to Landauer from Prague, on 21 November, 1937, trying to get a certificate and working place, is mentioned in Rautenberg-Alianov (2013), Personal Collection.

Figure 18: A former lawyer and his wife with their first baby-chicken, Ramot Hashavim (No year mentioned). Courtesy of the Central Zionist Archives

Most middle-class immigrants experienced deterioration in living standards, but measured by local standards of the quite poor Palestinian Jewish middle class and against the backdrop of the ethos of pioneering, this deterioration was not discernible. Moreover, the contribution of the immigrants to the development of the Palestinian economy added an important component to their own self esteem as successful immigrants.

Distinct Cultural Characteristics of the German Immigrants

With the assistance of the world Jewish immigration machinery, Palestine attracted people who had never before identified themselves with, or felt affinity to Jewish nationalism of any kind.[10] The first who immigrated to Palestine were veteran Zionists and youngsters who had already completed their training in agriculture, but they were soon joined by "new" Zionists who joined in their thousands the Zionist movement in order to become eligible for immigration certificates distributed by the JA. It is reasonable to assume that these new Zionists did not come from among those who were totally estranged from Judaism, and not from among the "Non-Aryan Christians" (Nazi terminology for Jews converted to Christianity).[11]

German Jews immigrating to Palestine during the 1930s raised the proportion of German stock in the Jewish population of Palestine, from less than two percent in the beginning of the 1930s to about 12 percent by the end of the decade. About 75 percent of the immigrants from Germany settled in urban areas, mainly Haifa, Tel Aviv, and to a lesser degree in Jerusalem, while some 25 percent settled in rural areas.[12] This urban-rural mix was essentially similar to the entire Jewish population of Palestine (73.6 percent of the Jews resided in urban localities in both 1931 and 1946 censuses).[13] A distinct spatial feature of the German-Jewish immigrants settling in towns was, however, their concentration in certain neighborhoods, such as Ben Yehuda Street in Tel Aviv, Rehavya in Jerusalem, and Ahuza on Mt. Carmel, in Haifa, which became identified as *Yekke* neighborhoods.

While the spatial concentration of immigrant groups enabling them to gain from network advantages and reduce the cost of adjustment to the new environment and language is a well-known phenomenon, within the Jewish immigrant society of Palestine it was particularly prominent and visible among the newcomers from Germany. In addition to the general factors shaping the enclaves of immigrants in receiving countries, the "German-specific" pattern in Palestine may have reflected the high language barrier and the cultural differences that distanced the German Jews from the rest of the Jewish society composed mainly of Eastern European Jews, and led to their self-imposed isolation.[14]

The German-Jewish immigrants were distinguished, already in the 1920s, by a high proportion of people with academic training.[15] They were mostly young, had just taken their first steps in their academic careers, but managed already

---

10 JA (1939).

11 Although there were some exceptions, as demonstrated in the study of Adi Gordon on the German weekly *Orient* in Palestine: Gordon (2004).

12 Gelber (1990), 344.

13 Based on tables 24–27 in *Population* (1962), and on table 1.2 in Bachi (1974).

14 Betten and Du-Nur (2000) also deal with the difficulties in adapting to the Hebrew language.

15 According to Gelber (1990), 57 (table based on JA data), the rate of professionals alone was about 20 percent.

to play a decisive role in building the infrastructure for the nascent academia within the *Yishuv* – the Hebrew University of Jerusalem, the Technion in Haifa, and the Sieff (Weizmann) Institute in Rehovot. This was a natural development reinforced by the fact that German academia was the intellectual habitus for a whole generation of Jewish academics originating in Eastern and Central Europe. Note that almost all Jewish academics involved in Palestine's academic life had been trained in German universities.[16] Moreover, the German-Jewish interwar immigrants made the Hebrew University the world center of Jewish studies for many years to come.

The transfer of German-Jewish medical people (between 1933 and 1939, some 1,200 physicians immigrated from Germany to Palestine), combined with the import of new technologies, chemical and other medicine-related industries also had a profound impact in Palestine, which needed German input to modernize its entire system of health services, both in public and private sectors. The same holds for the import of new professions and the introduction of new modern approaches, such as in social work, psychology and psychiatry, to the most advanced European professional standards, to which Palestine adapted itself. The number of immigrant doctors of all specializations grew dramatically until the end of 1935. At a certain point, though, the Palestine government restricted the entrance of physicians due to a growing surplus that caused unemployment among doctors.[17]

The Central European immigrants (not just the Germans but also those who came from Austria and Czechoslovakia) brought and implemented new standards and concepts of cultural demand and consumption. The Philharmonic Orchestra could have been founded much earlier than 1936 on the basis of available fine musicians among East European immigrants. But an enterprise like that could have succeeded only with sufficient potential subscribers, who became available with the arrival of the immigrants from Germany. The new demand for aesthetic standards in production and marketing gave a crucial push to the development of new artistic specializations, such as lithography and metal work which were introduced in the Bezalel Art Academy, and to musical education, performance, distribution and consumption. Many artistic professionals introduced modernist trends, such as in the realm of photography.[18]

Among the German immigrants were a high percentage of teachers. It may be assumed that Jewish teachers preferred Palestine, where they could utilize their

---

16 *Toldot Ha'Universita* (1997–2013).
17 Golz (2013, 2009); Lavsky (2003); Niederland (1996); Rolnik (2007); *Zalashik (2008)*.
18 Gelber (1990), 466–472; Helman (2007), 24–25, 163–164, 176–178; Ofrat (1987); Schloer (1995).

training. They also founded some of the most prominent schools, both religious and secular – Moriya and *Tikhon Hadash* in Tel Aviv, *Hugim* and Leo Baeck in Haifa, *Ma'ale* and *Horev* in Jerusalem. This fascinating subject of German-Jewish contribution has not yet been sufficiently investigated.[19]

Modernization in terms of religion was a failure. Germany was the cradle of the Liberal Conservative and Reform movements, and German Orthodoxy developed the "*Torah im Derech Eretz*" movement, which sought to combine tradition with modern intellectual and cultural European trends. Orthodox immigrants founded their synagogues – *Horev* in Jerusalem, *Ichud Shivat Zion* in Tel Aviv, *Ahavat Torah* in Haifa, and *Mekor Hayim* in Petah Tikva. The Liberals established *Emet Ve'Emunah* in Jerusalem and *Bet Israel* in Haifa.[20] But these religious innovations did not find any echo in Palestine, dominated entirely by Eastern European and Sephardic religious traditions. Only small congregations, made up by German worshippers in the three main cities, existed in isolation, with no impact on public religious customs.

The Encounter with the *Yishuv* and Organizational-Political Responses

German immigrants to Palestine experienced cultural shock encountering a strange mixture of Arabic-Oriental and Eastern European civilizations, which seemed to them inferior to their own culture.[21] This shock may have offset somewhat the comparative economic advantage of the immigrants, and may have added a special factor to their organizational behavior.

Arriving en masse in Palestine the German Jewish group encountered a wall of alienation. Several factors contributed to this. They came from a highly developed modern country, many of them from large urban centers, capitalists, businessmen, industrialists, professionals and academics. Their concentration in specific neighborhoods was not welcomed by the *Yishuv* and emphasized their strangeness and aloofness. The language barrier was decisive. Although a minority of the immigrants had studied Hebrew before arriving or grew up in religious homes with traditional Hebrew, the transfer from a European language to a Semitic language undergoing a rapid process of modernization was particularly difficult. Moreover, those coming from the German cultural circles arrived with

---

19 An exception is Niederland (2004).
20 Shashar (1997).
21 Getter (1979); Miron (2005).

confidence in the superiority of the German culture and language – the cradle of great human spiritual creativity in modern times.[22] In addition, there was a huge gap in cultural norms relating to the public sphere between cleanliness, politeness, punctuality, perfectionism, and aesthetics, versus the mixture of Eastern European-Levantine norms, which caused mutual reluctance and isolation, and even snobbism on the part of the newcomers.[23]

The feeling of superiority gained additional strength from the professional and academic status of the immigrants, their new standards in cultural consumption and creativity, and their contribution to the cultural and economic development of the country.

The encounter between the immigrants and the *Yishuv* was also tightly connected with the legacy of German Zionism. Of course, the wave of immigration was not dictated by ideology, but the Zionist organization paved the way and constructed the machinery, and the veteran Zionist leaders who came to Palestine were the ones who laid the foundations of the immigrants' organization, the HOG, which was not welcomed: "I cannot recall any convention of *histadrut* (organization) of Polish origin or Russian origin...Principally there is no East, or West, there are only Jews..."[24] The model of *Landsmannschaft*, common in the U.S.A. from the time of the mass Jewish migration at the turn of the 19th-20th centuries was meant to create a warm and familiar environment for the individual immigrant and thus to facilitate the road to integration into the larger society. This model was not endorsed by the all-Jewish *Yishuv* because it seemed to contradict the Zionist intention to gather dispersed Jews and to create a united nation.

However, the HOG differed from the familiar model of the *Landsmannschaft*. On the one hand it acted out of Zionist motivation and aimed at providing Zionist education to all German immigrants and to train them for the service of the national enterprise.[25] On the other hand it meant to empower the German-Jewish legacy of the immigrants group and to introduce it into the Palestinian culture and society. Hence, from its start the HOG nurtured its character as a political Zionist organization that would become a bridge between German Zionism and the *Yishuv*.

As already discussed, the achievements of the HOG proved to be successful in mobilizing and actually running the enterprise of absorption and settlement of

---

22 Lavsky (2009).

23 Greif et al. (2000), based on 80 interviews conducted between 1996–1999, most of them with immigrants from Germany.

24 From the opening speech of the *Histadrut* General Secretary David Remez at the *Histadrut* convention in 1935, cited in Deutsche Alijah (1935).

25 Marburg (2000), Personal Collection.

the German immigrants. This achievement was particularly remarkable against the background of the poor care taken by Zionist institutions on behalf of absorption in general.[26]

A unique feature of the Jewish community in Palestine was the combination of being semi-independent and benefiting from the Zionist immigration machinery. The German-Jewish immigrants, especially those who came from the ranks of the Zionist movement, could thus easily integrate into a Jewish-Zionist framework, with which many of them were quite familiar. Familiarity with the Zionist political and social setting dominated by Eastern European culture and persons on the one hand, and their own cultural heritage and pride on the other hand, sharpened the self-confidence and sense of superiority of the German-Jewish immigrants, and propelled their ambition to alter the political culture and public life in Jewish Palestine.

However, in the political sphere, German Zionists did not acquire the same position as in the realm of economic and social issues. Being immersed in the political atmosphere which dominated intellectual circles in the postwar Weimar Republic, German Zionists developed political skepticism. They refrained from political sectarian involvement, which in their view was bound with corruption and destined to harm the basic values of ideology as such. Therefore they tended to compromise, to unify, to keep together with a broad consensus. German Zionist leaders did not participate in Zionist party politics, but remained loyal to the WZO President Chaim Weizmann and concentrated on matters relating to the building up of Palestine, and it was this realm in which they played a decisive role.

Having nurtured the moderate liberal legacy of rationalism and universal humanism, German Zionists sought to implant these virtues in their Zionist worldview. Many leaders of the German Zionist movement were active in shaping the Brit Shalom Association that supported the bi-national idea as the right way to solve the Arab-Jewish conflict. However, precisely this dominance of the compromising political attitude prevented them from penetrating the world Zionist political leadership. In view of the success in mobilizing the absorption enterprise and in their cultural role and impact, HOG leaders and activists felt disappointed in their failure to take the same central position in Zionist political leadership. The cultural-language barrier was also an obstacle in the sphere of social and political culture – between their tolerant liberal legacy and that which characterized the Eastern European legacy of party politics. They differed in their wish to create a consensus above party politics in their compromising attitude regarding the

---

26 Lavsky (2003).

Arab-Jewish conflict, and in their support of a middle way between socialism and capitalism. The HOG leaders were all former Zionist activists in Germany, and the ZVfD was to a great extent affiliated with the Zionist world leadership identified with Weizmann.[27] Thus, they felt that they should be welcomed into the *Yishuv*'s leadership – which did not happen.

Indeed, the political dimension was embedded in HOG, and from 1933, led by the Zionist leader and former Chair of the ZVfD Kurt Blumenfeld, it established its German organ *Mitteilungsblat*, which served as a platform for the Zionist immigrants expressing their various views about a broad range of issues concerning Zionism, the *Yishuv* and world politics, but refrained from further steps toward political party organization. In the political arena in which they had acted in Germany there was a clear distinction between three political circles – the general German polity, in which each one voted for the party he chose; the German-Jewish community, in which all Zionists appeared as a united party, and the World Zionist Organization, in which the ZVfD appeared as a pro-Weizmann unity, based on a broad consensus. This distinction enabled German Zionists to act as a united front as long as the WZO was led by Weizmann – the "General Zionist." The HOG did not recognize, however, the principal difference between the political arena in which they had acted in Germany and the one to which they should adapt themselves in Palestine, where there was only one circle, the Jewish Zionist-organized community, led by the Zionist labor leader, David Ben-Gurion. Thus they insisted on presenting a united political front in the municipal elections, and continued to call for united consensual political organization, above and beyond the existing Zionist party politics. After a decade of political frustration they eventually founded in 1942 a political party of their own, "*Aliya Hadasha*" (New Immigration). This *Landsmannschaft* party, led by Felix Rosenblüth and Georg Landauer, represented the moderate pro-Leftist legacy of German Zionism and appeared as opposition to the Zionist leadership. Despite short term success (winning the second place in the elections of 1944 to the *Yishuv*'s parliament, *Asefat Hanivharim*) it caused a split within the group of German immigrants, never gained supporters outside their circles, and existed for barely six years. However, its offspring, the Progressive Party, played a significant role in the politics of Israel during the first decade of statehood, and Felix Rosenblüth (Pinhas Rosen) served as the first Israeli Minister of Justice.[28]

---

27 Lavsky (1996).
28 Bondy (1990); Gelber (1987); Getter (1982); Lavsky (2014); Yishai (1981).

Conclusion

The encounter between Palestine and the immigrants from Germany was a successful encounter from the point of view of the Palestine Jewish community, which gained enormously from the German-Jewish input in the cultural and economic spheres. German immigrants, despite their successful economic integration and cultural contribution, had little impact on the political system, and in political life of the National Home and Israel. From the point of view of the immigrants, economic success was accompanied by cultural, social and political alienation and inundated with a sense of superiority and frustration that persisted for many years to come.

Chapter 8
Encounter and Integration in the United States

Economic Aspects

The huge wave of exiled Central European academics, intellectuals and artists in the first years of the Nazi regime attracted much attention in the international arena and in the U.S. and aroused a concerted initiative to assist and receive them. For that matter the Academic Assistance Council and other aid committees were established by American academics, with the assistance of voluntary financing, especially by the Rockefeller Foundation. Many chairs and teaching posts were thus founded in order to place the newcomers. An outstanding initiative was that of Alvin Johnson, the director of the New School experimental institution for adult education in New York to transform it, in 1933, into the New School for Social Sciences ("University in Exile") in New York, which absorbed about 180 scholars from Central Europe.[1] Despite many concerns of various interest groups, the academics who were among the first to immigrate to the U.S. were accepted and integrated into the American academic and artistic establishment. They were the most successful and visible, were active in all disciplines, introduced notable innovations and in some fields contributed greatly to upgrading American arts and sciences. They were also the most articulate in writing and documenting their experiences, and attracted the attention of scholars dealing with the Nazi era immigration to the U.S.[2]

Although the German-Jewish immigration to the United States included some of the most integrated and prosperous members of the German-Jewish community, the majority who arrived at the end of the 1930s were forced to leave behind most if not all of their possessions, which left them at a material disadvantage.[3]

As a result of the public concern regarding this immigration wave, the Committee for the Study of Recent Immigration from Europe was organized in 1944, by five leading national refugee service organizations, to conduct a nation-wide investigation, based on individual and communal questionnaires:[4]

---

1 Krohn (1993).
2 See for instance: Brinkmann and Wolff (1999); Coser (1984); Epstein (1993); Hagemann and Krohn (1999); Hassler and Wertheimer (1997); Heilbut (1997); Hughes (1975); Lehmann (1991); Strauss (1987); Traber and Weingarten (1987).
3 Fields (1938); Grebler (1976).
4 Davie and Koenig (1945), 2; the full report: Davie (1947), the citation hereafter is taken from the introduction, xi.

DOI 10.1515/9783110501650-009

The recent refugee movement to the United States has aroused unusual interest because of its dramatic character, the type of people it involved, and the international unrest characterizing the period when it occurred. Composed primarily of middle- and upper-class persons, it contrasted sharply with earlier immigration movements and attracted the interest and sometimes the opposition of American professional and business people who hitherto had seldom if ever been directly concerned with immigrant arrivals as associates or competitors. Since a majority of the refugees were either Jews by confession or "non-Aryans," that is, Jews by descent only, the movement provided a basis for anti-Semitic agitation, which was intensified by German propaganda. The refugees became the object of widespread discussion. On the one hand, they were hailed as a superior group greatly enriching American cultural and economic life and, on the other hand, as a destructive and subversive element in our society.

What are the facts? How many of our recent immigrants have been refugees? To what nationalities and religious groups do they belong? How have our immigration laws functioned during this period, and how have they been administered? Where have the refugees settled? How have they adjusted themselves to American life? What do they think of Americans? What do Americans think of them? What is their attitude toward assimilation? Do they intend to remain or to return? What effect have they had on American society? What contributions have they made to our culture and economy? In short, have they been an asset or a liability to this country?

These reports enable us to follow the process of the various aspects of integration experienced by the immigrants.

The road to economic integration was particularly hard for those who came to the United States in the years immediately before the war. These refugees suffered confiscation of property and were allowed after 1937 to take out only 10 Reichs marks in currency. The great majority of them thus arrived without funds. Often they had to take menial jobs at first, and many had not found employment consonant with their former positions. The typical refugee lost all signs of his rank and had to regain them under completely changed circumstances. Persons who had been independent became dependent on others. The need to do hard physical labor, to which they were unaccustomed, was especially trying to middle aged and older people. When asked what was the greatest change in their immigration experience the most frequent answer was the change in occupation.[5]

However, nearly two fifths of the refugees who had been business proprietors or managers in Europe continued as such in the United States, while a fourth of them obtained employment in allied fields as clerks, bookkeepers, agents and salesmen. Nearly one half of those who had been clerical and office workers in Europe found employment in that category. About one third became manual laborers in industry, in addition to those who came already as skilled and semi-skilled workers. Many of them did eventually advance to white-collar jobs.

---

5 Davie (1947), 120.

Especially large number of the refugees became self-employed or employed as butchers and bakers, or in factories, and some found employment in businesses started earlier by German Jews. Many tried to establish themselves in business, operating from their apartments. Many shops were specialty shops: furniture polish, candy, upholstery, slipcovers, watches, dress, hats, toys, machine-repair, barbering, wholesale coffee, chocolate, jewelry, bookbinding. Some of the products were invented by the entrepreneurs and manufactured in their apartments. These kinds of small businesses relied on the demand and taste of German clientele: bakeries, perfumes, medicines, syrup, restaurants and cafeterias, chess and card clubs, wedding chapels, home-cooked lunches and suppers. These apartment businesses were often run by women.[6]

Many refugees showed great ingenuity in starting new types of businesses. They brought with them and developed new processes and manufacture of new products formerly unknown or imported, such as scientific instruments, precision tools and synthetic industrial products. Many manufacturers produced articles essential to the war effort. The German-Jewish immigrant group was a labor-creating group: opened factories and shops and introduced new processes and products.

The Committee for the Study of Recent Immigration from Europe, in collaboration with the American Federation of Jews from Central Europe, took a sample of 158 refugee-owned manufacturing concerns: 69 of these were producing goods not previously manufactured in the U.S., 50 had introduced new products, 22 new processes, 16 new patents, 7 secret formulas, 13 new skills – this for the period up to 1946.[7]

A few typical stories: Mr. S. had been an exporter in Germany. He lived in comfortable circumstances. He was arrested and put on trial and would have been imprisoned but managed to escape and after months of wandering reached the shores of the United States and encountered a foreign country. His English was poor, so he decided to learn English by mingling with local people. He started as a peddler, selling candy that his wife made. He then tried jobs offered to him by various agencies but he felt that as a businessman he wanted to start his own business. After a year and a half, and after talking to many local businesspeople and receiving their advice, he bought a small defense plant in a New England town with the financial help of another German refugee. He settled down and lived modestly, far below his former luxurious life, but was satisfied and felt integrated as an American.[8]

---

6 Lowenstein (1989), Chapter 3.

7 Hirshler (1955), 89–100.

8 Davie and Koenig (1945), 1–2, brings the story as a typical illustration.

Within a short while after coming to Indianapolis, Mr. C., formerly a store owner in Germany, secured a position as salesman with a national chain department store. Within five years he gradually elevated himself to the position of buyer in men's furnishing department.[9]

In some professions, particularly in medicine, the United States proved less welcoming. The worst case was that of dentists, since American dentistry was the most advanced in the world and the dentistry guild was extremely rigid.[10] The physicians were the largest single group of professionals among the refugees (5,000). Approximately three fourths of them were specialists in one branch or another. Under pressure from powerful professional associations, the authorities of most states imposed strict requirements for studies and examinations as prerequisites for authorizing immigrant physicians to practice medicine. Many of the immigrant doctors settled in New York City due to the fact that New York State required only former citizenship papers of applicants for the licensing examinations. However, many physicians either failed the examinations, or had to give up their special medical branch to become general practitioners. Many were too old to cope with all the requirements and prerequisites in a new language and thus had to adjust to other available jobs or to abandon employment altogether.[11]

A striking example of the way doctors coped with the hardships facing them as latter-day refugees is the case of the couple Erich and Hertha Nathorff, both well-established physicians from Berlin, he as an internist and she as a pediatrician.[12] The couple had barely managed to get permission to immigrate to America after Erich had been released from his imprisonment in Dachau at the end of 1938. After sending their son to England the couple managed to emigrate from Germany in April 1939, reunite with their son and arrive together in New York early in 1940:

> The two nights with my cousin were dreary and full of torment...Thanks to an acquaintance we happened to run into, we have found accommodations in a "Shelter for the Homeless"... (February 25, 1940).[13]...The hoop-jumping has begun again, by which I mean the trips I have to make to various organizations in order to get advice and assistance... above all to find a work... the counselors are partly true-born Americans who speak only English, partly emigrants [sic] who arrived a few years earlier than us, encountered fewer difficulties, and act as if they don't understand a word of German.... We arrived completely destitute. And the hope

---

9 Davie (1947), 142.

10 Dr. Henry Smith Leiper: Those German Refugees – facts do not justify the propaganda about refugees displacing American jobholders (May 1939), in Chamberlain Archives, YIVO, RG 278, Box 4.

11 Bentwich (1936), 183; Davie and Koenig (1945), 20–21; Fields (1938), 125.

12 Nathorff (1987), translated excerpts of it appeared under the title "A Doctor's View" in Anderson (1998) from which the following citations are taken.

13 Anderson (1998), 216.

that we would at least get the container with all our belongings out of hock.... now appears illusory. When I finally made this clear to the social worker, she said to me: "You want to be a doctor again? Get that crazy idea out of your head. We have enough doctors here, we don't want any more, and especially not any lady doctors. Your husband and you should take a job as domestic housekeepers. That way you'll have a roof over your heads, some food in your stomachs and on top of it you'll have a salary and can start saving" (February 27, 1940).[14]

Indeed she got a domestic job, moving from one household to another and rented a "miserable room" for all three of them. In the meantime, the husband Erich started studying English. In June 5, 1940 she writes: "My husband has passed his language exam... I myself have just had some luck. I start tomorrow as a night nurse in a hospital."[15] Having passed his New York State Medical Examination, Erich set up in February 1941 a practice on Central Park West. Hertha began slowly to develop a new career as a social worker and psychotherapist, based on her experience as a woman immigrant working with new immigrants, but never returned to her original profession as a pediatrician.[16] Her diary not only reveals the troubles of settling down but also represents the decisive role played by women in adjusting to new circumstances, paving the road for their husbands' renewed careers and their flexibility in building their own new careers.

Other immigrant professionals had difficulties as well. Teachers found it almost impossible to adjust to the educational system in English, and just gave up their former occupation. As for lawyers – they experienced the greatest difficulties in making use of their special skills that had been developed in the German legal system. Most of them abandoned their profession and integrated in various jobs in business and industry.[17] For example, a middle-aged lawyer from Germany adjusted himself by becoming a salesman in Los Angeles. He was successful and became a representative for the West Coast.[18]

There were also German-Jewish immigrants who made a complete revolution in their professional lives, and established themselves as farmers in various parts of the U.S.A. This was the case, for example of George Anker, a former business-man in Berlin, who arrived in the U.S. with his family in 1940. The family settled in Van Nuys, California, where Georg established a chicken farm.[19]

---

14 Anderson (1998), 216–217.
15 Anderson (1998), 220–221.
16 Anderson (1998), 299. See also her collection at the Center for Jewish History, New York.
17 Davie and Koenig (1945), 23–24.
18 Davie (1947), 142.
19 United States Holocaust Memorial Museum, courtesy of George Fogelson (Collections: 2003.353, text accompanying photo 15286).

Figure 19: A German-Jewish refugee couple work on their chicken farm in Vineland, NJ. Courtesy of the U.S. Holocaust Memorial Museum.

This is how Davie and Koenig summed up in 1945 the economic integration of the refugees:

> The majority of the refugees ultimately found work in business and the professions, even though many of them were forced at first to accept menial jobs. Owing to the shortage of manpower during the war period, practically all of those seeking employment eventually found work. Often they did not find it in the occupation for which they were trained abroad. Yet practically all have become self-supporting. Among the few still needing financial assistance are those either too old or too young to work and the physically or emotionally handicapped... Most of the refugees... now feel their living conditions are as good as or better than those they enjoyed in Europe. This is particularly true of the skilled and unskilled workers, the younger persons, and those who have lived here a number of years. On the other hand, among the professionals and business people of the older age groups, and those who have been here a comparatively short time, the majority report their living conditions as being the same or worse.[20]

The last sentence cited makes it clear that the high level of success experienced by early immigrants was distinctly different from that of more recent immigrants, and those who had encountered many more hardships caused by their demographic and economic profiles and by the unwelcoming circumstances.[21]

Another typical trait of the German immigrants might be drawn along gender lines. Women refugees integrated more easily into the market. The largest group had been homemakers abroad, but they found it easier to find jobs. They accepted inferior types of work with more composure than men, to whom this meant a greater sense of loss and frustration. There was much demand for domestic assistance and practically no competition in this field. It seems also that women were much quicker in acquiring the language and adapting themselves to new customs. Men often pointed to the language barrier as their main problem in economic integration. This was probably due to their professional background, which did not allow them to be content with a superficial knowledge of the language. Moreover, women, who frequently became gainfully employed in the initial period, quickly adapted to the American surroundings and were much more flexible and compromising in using the language. About three fifths of the women refugees though became homemakers again after the initial emergency period.[22]

---

20 Davie and Koenig (1945), 14–15.
21 On the overall success in economic integration, see also: Hirsch and Hirsch (1961).
22 Davie and Koenig (1945), 33–34; Quack (1995); see also, Quack (1995a).

Between Identities: Americanization, Jewish Awareness and German Legacy

On the front page of the German-Jewish monthly *Aufbau* of 1 December, 1936, appeared an article titled *"Emigrantentum – Geistige Neuorientierung"* (Emigrationism – spiritual/mental reorientation).[23] The author starts with a well-known joke, telling about two German immigrants standing on the Fifth Avenue watching the Independence Day parade, when one turns to the other, remarking: "In Germany they parade much better." This joke, continues the author, expresses in a nutshell the common phenomenon of immigrants who always make comparisons in order to criticize the American society and culture as inferior to the German-European one. This typical elitist arrogant attitude of German immigrants is actually an expression of the inferiority complex of the refugee, who was forced to abandon his homeland. But its consequences are harmful. It denies the opportunity to transform from the status of refugee to that of an immigrant, and turns the initial welcoming attitude of the Americans into an antagonistic attitude, thus barring the road toward real adaptation and full integration by becoming proud and devoted new Americans.

Adopting the English language and accepting American norms and customs was the main social-cultural problem encountered by the new Americans, Jews and non-Jews, assimilated or traditional. Generally they tried to actively overcome the barriers for practical daily matters. However, they were not inclined to abandon their German or German-Jewish heritage.

The German-Jewish immigrants tended to concentrate mainly on the East coast, half of them in New York City. On the West Coast, Los Angeles became the main center, though there was considerable dispersal to other communities, large and small, around the country. In the East coast many settled in New Jersey, Pennsylvania, and Massachusetts; in the Mid-West, they settled especially in Ohio, Illinois, Wisconsin and Michigan.[24]

Although the immigrants did not usually concentrate in specific neighborhoods or form separate colonies, there were a few exceptions that did not represent the typical contours of the German-Jewish immigration. Manhattan's Washington Heights ("Frankfurt on the Hudson") was made up mainly of Orthodox Jews who came from small towns in southern Germany quite impoverished

---

23 http://archive.org/stream/aufbau1519341939germ#page/n0/mode/1up
24 Davie and Koenig (1945), 13; Fields (1938); Jay (1997); Krohn (1998), 460, notes that two thirds of the immigrants settled in New York City and that Los Angeles accounted for the second-largest concentration. See also Bahr (2007).

in the late 1930s. The reasons for the Orthodox German Jews to prefer Washington Heights is not completely clear. There are several explanations including the theory of the "chain migration," the physical layout of the area (parks and hills), the inexpensive housing and the large Jewish population. In any case, Washington Heights was atypical for the German-Jewish immigration in its social, cultural and economic structure. It did not include the cultural and economic elite of German Jewry and thus did not become the center of New York German Jewry.

Another example of urban concentration was Baltimore, where the German-Jewish immigrants settled in the middle-class area around Eustaw Place and Druid Hill Park and various other clusters developed within walking distance of Orthodox synagogues.[25]

Los Angeles was a special case. LA was a developing city, more open to new creativity. It was then a paradise – with clear air, no highways, and very cheap cost of living. LA was a garden city, an urban sprawl, becoming the seat of middle class and the most affluent center in the West, with neighborhoods such as Beverly Hills, Westwood, Santa Monica, Brentwood and Pacific Palisades. About 10,000 to 15,000 German immigrants came to southern California between 1933 and 1941, and about 70 percent of them were Jews. Many of them were first rank intellectuals – Theodor Adorno and Max Horkheimer, Herbert Marcuse and Alfred Doeblin. UCLA served as the elite's employment center. The Hollywood film industry was a focal attraction due to former close ties between the German and the American film industries. Hollywood established a special fund to absorb exiled professionals from Berlin and Vienna known for their innovative creativity in the field, and the immigrants themselves, men and women, like the author Wicky Baum, established a cooperative fund for mutual assistance. It is difficult to reconstruct the German-speaking exile community in LA of the 1930s and 1940s. Social history remains to be written.[26]

Despite initial concerns of veteran Americans, arising mainly out of economic considerations, the immigrants were rapidly accepted as full citizens and as another legitimate (albeit not new) sector in America's already heterogeneous society. Although, as mentioned, it is difficult to determine precisely the proportion of German Jews among total European Jewish immigration to the United States over the entire period, it may be assumed that Central European Jewish immigrants (including Austrian and Czech nationals) constituted the majority of

---

25 Davie and Koenig (1945), 14–15; Lowenstein (1989), Chapter 3; Weiner (2004), 18.

26 Horak (1986); Bahr (2007), introduction, 1–10. Bahr remarks that according to Gerald D. Nash (historian of the American West), the German immigrants made a profound cultural contribution. This is defined in terms of the cultural product with no reference to the community search for a social, political and religious identity and adaptation.

the "Hebrew" immigration to the United States between 1933 and 1941. Taking the figure of 129,000 as a reasonable upper limit for the Central European Jewish immigration during this period,[27] it may be inferred that this influx added only slightly more than three percent to the existing American Jewish population of 4,000,000 (in 1933).

What was specifically associated with the Jewish dimension of the Nazi era immigration, in the process of encounters and responses? Here again a distinction should be made between the elite and the masses. Generally, the Jewish cultural elite tended to assimilate, and was not distinguished particularly as Jewish, not in reality and not in the vast study of its cultural contribution to America.[28] The majority were interested in swift assimilation. This did not prevent identification with the German cultural heritage as the programs of the Jewish Club of 1933 indicate. They continued to conduct social lives among themselves and to speak German with each other.[29]

But what about the great majority of middle-class immigrants? Generally, the newcomers were relatively homogenous group, well educated, world minded and cultured – anxious to understand and contribute, yet critical. The immigrants themselves began to create organizations concerned mainly at first with occupational problems, later with caring for the aged and social activities (about 20 percent were over 60 years old in 1953). They drew together into their own social clubs, own religious congregations, separate religious organizations and the Conference of Jewish Immigrant Congregations. Old associations from Germany were renewed in America, professional societies and even university fraternities. Some joined the Zionist Theodor Herzl Club and the Maccabees, and formed a separate German Jewish Representative Committee in the World Jewish Congress.[30]

Moreover, on the basis of being recognized as deserving of special treatment, the newcomers readily constituted *Landsmannschaft*-type organizations, building on already existing groups and institutions. German-Jewish clubs and various associations, founded in the 1920s, served as models for the establishment of similar institutions during the 1930s (among them the German-Jewish Clubs in Los Angeles and New York that were founded in 1924 and 1934, respectively) to promote economic, social and cultural integration of the newcomers.

---

27 Davie and Koenig (1945), 3–11.

28 An exception is the attempt to address the Jewish dimension of the intellectual elite's impact on the American culture: Peck (1989).

29 Barron and Eckmann (1997) and Bahr (2007) with reference to the German colony on the West Coast.

30 Hirshler (1955), 89–100.

Membership,however, totaled only a few thousands, and these clubs lasted only for a few years.[31] The American Federation of Jews from Central Europe was established in 1941.[32]

New immigrants also founded German-language periodicals, the most important of them the *Aufbau*. The *Aufbau* (Construction) monthly was established in December 1934 by new immigrants under the auspices of the New York based German-Jewish Club on its tenth anniversary. In 1939 Manfred George (October 22, 1893 – December 30, 1965), a German journalist, author and translator, arrived penniless in the United States. He became the editor of *Aufbau* and transformed it from a small monthly newsletter into an important weekly newspaper, especially during World War II and the postwar era, when it became an important source of information for Jews trying to establish new lives, and for Nazi concentration camp survivors to find each other. George remained Editor in Chief of the *Aufbau* until his death. Within a few years the *Aufbau* expanded from 300 to 30,000 subscribers all over the U.S. and beyond. A special edition of the *Aufbau, Die Westküste* (The West Coast) appeared as a biweekly in Los Angeles.[33]

A survey of the *Aufbau* clearly reveals the integration process, its obstacles and limitations. The *Aufbau* envisaged its role in helping the immigrants to become good Americans, to encounter and make them familiar with social surroundings.[34] That said, it indeed fulfilled the double purpose of a virtual *Landsmannshaft*, cultivating Jewish and German heritage and communal ties, and at the same time leaning toward full integration in the American society. Thus, almost each issue contained a full page in English out of an average of 10 pages, encouraged the readers to take English lessons advertised in the paper and published lots of useful information about American norms of shopping, university life, etc. At the same time, the *Aufbau* gave much space to advertisements of German restaurants and shops, to articles about great German intellectuals, and particularly reported about Jewish tradition and cultural events organized by the German-Jewish Club in New York. Many issues included articles relating to Jewish history and tradition, and the Jewish world, particularly Zionist policy and the

---

31 German-Jewish Club, LBIANY, AR 6466; *Aufbau*, Year 1, no. 1, Dec. 1, 1934, front page.
32 American Federation of Jews from Central Europe, Inc., *Ten Years, 1941–1951* (New York), LBIANY.
33 Krohn (1998); about Manfred George in http://en.wikipedia.org/wiki/Manfred_George (accessed July 28, 2014).
34 *Aufbau*, 1/1, December 11,1934, front page, celebrating 10 years of the German-Jewish Club; issue 3/4, March 1937.

national home in Palestine.[35] Of course, the *Aufbau* gave much space to international and American policy regarding the Nazi regime, deplored the rigid American immigration policy and reported extensively about German immigration to the U.S. and its dispersion. With the outbreak of WWII, efforts were taken to convince the Americans that German Jews should not be seen as "enemy aliens," e.g., the *Aufbau* added in November 1939 the subtitle: "dedicated to the Americanization of the immigrants."

It should be reiterated that a large German presence in American Jewry was established during the 19th century, although German Jews' proportion in the American Jewish population was later minimized by the massive immigration of Eastern European Jews from 1880 to 1914. Nevertheless, German Jews had imported already in the 19th century German-Jewish traditions, and significantly shaped certain areas of American Jewish life, notably in the realm of liberal religious trends and the Jewish philanthropic and welfare organizations. Jews of German background maintained their hegemonic position in national Jewish affairs until after World War I.

By the 1930s, however, leadership positions were increasingly occupied by well- established Jews of Eastern European origin.[36] Given this background, the impact of the immigration from Nazi Germany on both the American Jewish community and on its German-origin component was rather limited. The new immigrants arrived at a time when the American Jewish populace was already dominated by Eastern European Jews. Moreover, American Jewry had long since adopted various German-Jewish cultural and religious patterns.

In the Jewish religious context, the arrival of the newcomers was barely noticeable. The Conservative and Reform movements were already well established, along with their respective educational systems. Newcomers could easily find synagogues suitable to their tradition and could send their children to public or existing Jewish day schools. There were, however, differences in customs, liturgy and manners between German and Eastern European Orthodox congregations. There were cases in which a rabbi from Germany formed an independent congregation for his fellow refugees – Simon Schwab of Ischenhausen, for instance, who moved to Baltimore and took up the post of rabbi of Congregation Shearith Israel, which soon became the center of German-Jewish observant refugees who gravitated to the neighborhood of this "Glen Avenue shul."[37]

---

35 An outstanding illustration is the issue of June 1, 1936 that published three articles in this context: Erich de Jonge, *"Eretz Israel oder Panarabism,"* Robert Stricker, *"Warum brauchen wir den Judenstaat,"* and Clara Simons on Kibbutz Bet Alpha. This was probably a response to the Arab Rebellion and the nomination of the Peel Commission on the Palestine Mandate.

36 Feingold (1992); Shapiro (1971).

37 Deter (2004), 11; Weiner (2004), 18.

Alongside these sectorial activities, many of the immigrant influx actively sought to join veteran American organizations and institutions, acquire the English language, and mix socially and professionally with non-immigrants. Younger immigrants and women among them, in particular, succeeded in learning the ropes. This was atypical for immigrants and refugees, comparatively speaking. The devotion, persistence and systematic strategies employed by the immigrants to attain civic integration may have had their roots in German cultural models; but these patterns could also have been based on their high professional level, the familiarity some of them already had with English and with other features of American culture, and the fact that many of them chose to settle down in established American neighborhoods rather than in tight immigrant clusters.[38] Thus, most of them did not wait too long to start the process of naturalization even before the war. Others who may have hesitated did so during the war. When the U.S. entered the war, many new immigrants volunteered, and their German skills served the occupying forces by the end of the war and thereafter.[39]

Conclusion

The new immigrants from Germany may be divided in two sectors whose entrance to the U.S. occurred at different times, and their experiences, as well as their acceptance and impact were largely different. On the one hand the minority, comprised of the cultural German elite, had a profound impact on American intellectual and cultural life and maintained its own self-identification as Europeans and Germans. The majority of the immigrants who came late, as refugees, had to overcome the economic and cultural challenges and to find their place. With the assistance of their predecessors they constructed a network of virtual *Landsmannschaft* and did their utmost to become Americans. It seems that in the long run they did well without leaving a profound mark or creating a unique or visible component in the pluralistic American society, nor did they add something new to the American Jewish community. Their contribution to America's social, intellectual and cultural spheres was of a broad and universal nature rather than being distinctly German Jewish.

---

38 Davie and Koenig (1945), 15. The extent to which these patterns influenced relationships between Eastern European Jews and the German-Jewish newcomers has yet to be carefully explored.
39 NARA, RG 59, Table: American servicemen in World War II: 9,550 Jewish refugees from Germany. Many scattered testimonies on becoming American citizens, and on enlisting to the army, for example: Testimony of Siegfried Rosenthal (ME 962 MM II 21), LBIANY Archives. See also Davie and Koenig (1945), 18–19.

Chapter 9
Encounter and Integration in Britain

Economic Aspects

Within the overall negative attitude toward immigration, the British government encouraged the immigration and absorption of industrialists from Germany, and acted in this direction under the pressure of public opinion and the labor unions, as expressed by the British Home Secretary in 1936 apologetically:

> In point of fact there has been little hostility to the policy of rigid but sympathetic control exercised by the Home Office, with the result that several thousand desirable, industrious, intelligent and acceptable persons have been added to the population. They have brought with them considerable capital, and established industries which already have given employment to more British subjects than the total number of refugees from Germany who are now living in the United Kingdom.[1]

However, the great majority of immigrants arrived by the end of the 1930s and held a variety of occupations with no relevance to the British economy. They could not hold to their former vocations. On the contrary, many of them came with special labor permits issued in favor of manual works or for training. For example, Max Abraham (born 1913), a craftsman and teacher at an ORT school, arrived three days before the war broke out and was sent to Kitchener Camp, where he looked after his pupils.[2] Frank William Henderson, born 1916, worked as a secretary in a lawyer's office. After the Nazis forced him out of work in 1935 he went to Berlin to undertake a training course so that he could find work abroad. The director of the course organized for about 20 boys to go to England to help get the Kitchener Camp ready, but they had to make their own travel arrangements. He arrived in England in March 1939 but had to make his own way to the camp. There he had to get a hospital section ready within 24 hours and then worked with the doctor.[3] Willy Hirschfeld, born 1920 in Bonn, worked in a metal factory in Siegburg, and was arrested on 10 November, 1938, at the factory. Taken prisoner in Cologne he was then deported to Dachau concentration camp. He was released from Dachau in April 1939 and came to the U.K. on an agricultural permit, which was arranged

---

1 Cited in: Mock (1986), 78.
2 Interview with Max Abraham, 21 March, 2003, WLL, Refugee Voices, no. 10.
3 Interview with Frank William Henderson, 3 May, 2004, Refugee Voices, no. 60.

DOI 10.1515/9783110501650-010

for him through his former boss, who had emigrated earlier, and with the help of the Jewish Refugee Committee, as he described it:

> It was an agricultural permit – that I can only work in England on the farm, learn the trade and, eventually would be sent to Palestine at the time. But, as the war started, there was no going to Palestine or anything else... So, when we arrived in Harwich, we took the train to Liverpool Street Station and there was my boss waiting for us to take us to his house... The next day when I was taken to the Bloomsbury House where all the refugees had to report and from there you were told where to go.[4]

One of the most available entry opportunities for women was the domestic visa, issued by the Labour Office to supply demand by British families for housekeeping jobs. About 20,000 refugee women from Germany, Austria and Czechoslovakia came this way to England before the war.[5] Among the 97 interviews with refugees from Germany, six came to England on a domestic visa. Inge Ader was born Inge Nord in 1918. After facing discrimination at school, she decided she wanted to become a photographer and started an apprenticeship in photography. She passed her exams in 1937 and started working as a photographer. She came on a domestic visa to the U.K. in 1939 but eventually opened her own photographic studio.[6] Elisabeth Bernstein, born 1920, was trained in domestic jobs and in June 1939 went as a domestic to the family of a missionary, who were on holiday in Edinburgh. She travelled via Hamburg to Leigh. She was happy to have left Germany and was happy with the family. When they left Edinburgh, she went to her aunt and uncle in Leicester, who found her a position with a Jewish family in Leicester.[7]

Lillian Heyman, nee Liselotte Rosl Lachmann, was born 1919 in Berlin. She left school at 16 to train as a window-dresser and worked in a big department store. Her future husband, Ernest Heyman, who had been in the U.K. since 1936, put an advertisement for a domestic position in the papers. Lillian came to the U.K. in February 1939 on a domestic visa. She later found work as a window-dresser.[8]

Most of the late-comers had to go through a long period of economic hardship in finding work and worked in manual or other lowly jobs, typical for refugee migrants, who have to adjust themselves to a new economy and start anew. However, in the case of Britain, the path to economic and social integration of the German immigrants was decidedly influenced by the fact that the great majority arrived close to the British declaration of war against Germany, on 3 September,

4 Interview with Willy Hirschfeld, 17 June, 2003, Refugee Voices, no. 21.

5 Davidson (1991); Kushner (1991).

6 Interview with Inge Ader, 4 and 11 June, 2003, WLL, Refugee Voices, no. 18 (S).

7 Interview with Elisabeth Bernstein, 29 July, 2005, Refugee Voices, no. 27 (N).

8 Interview with Lillian Heyman, 4 December, 2006, Refugee Voices, no. 141 (S).

1939. Thus, the British government, always suspicious of aliens, now fearful of pro-German trends, immediately introduced the category of Enemy Alien to its treatment of newcomers. All the refugees were now divided between three grades of Enemy Aliens: The majority (71,600 out of 73,400, namely 90 percent) were classified C – those regarding whom there was no doubt about their loyalty to Britain; B category applied to those regarding whom the tribunals cast some doubts, and they were restricted in entering areas of employment and residence; to Category A belonged all those regarding whom the tribunals had serious doubts. The persons under category A were interned in the Isle of Man, or deported for internment to Canada and Australia.[9]

The internment and restrictions became a great obstacle on the way to economic integration, let alone social and cultural adaptation. Let us follow a few stories exemplifying the twisted road toward integration.

Frank William Henderson, who arrived in 1939 in the Kitchener Camp, stayed there for three months and then went to Manchester, where he had a friend, and then to London. Through the Refugee Committee he found odd jobs for a while and lived in a hostel. He found a job with Levinsons, the wine people, filling bottles of wine for Passover. After Passover 1940 he was fired. He went to work for a cotton mill in Oldham repairing the machines but was interned as an Enemy Alien in June 1940 in Whitchurch. In October he was released and commandeered into the Pioneer Corps building Nissan Huts in Shropshire and in Stafford.[10]

Willy Hirschfeld, who came on an agricultural permit, went to report to Bloomsbury House:

> They told me I should go – they gave me a railway ticket, and told me I should go to a farm near Bude. A beautiful place, I must say! I was very well looked after at this farm. The farmer was a very nice man and even asked me if he could help my parents to come to England... Unfortunately, after three months (I don't know when the war started – in September, didn't it?) I was told I cannot stay there anymore because it was a restricted area or a protected area. They sent me to a farm in Sussex and this was a dreadful place.
>
> When I arrived in London I had no money at all so I went to the Bloomsbury House again and they told me off terribly. "You can't just disappear. You can't do that." So I told them how dreadfully I was treated, so they said, "What do you want to do now?" Well, I have got to find myself work in London and they gave me coupons to stay at a Rowton House in Whitechapel. You know what a Rowton House is in Whitechapel? A Rowton House is a place where, for one shilling, you can stay the night. You get a blanket. It is where all down-and-outs stay. So I got three shillings so I could stay three nights. I got myself a job

---

9 The saga of detention on the Isle of Man and deportation to Australia and Canada has been dealt with extensively. See for example: Stent (1980).
10 Interview with Frank William Henderson, 4 May, 2004, WLL, Refugee Voices, no. 60.

Figure 20: Cover to a program for a Passover Seder held in the Hotel Ramsey, Mooragh Internment Camp on the Isle of Man, April 1940. Courtesy of the U.S. Holocaust Memorial Museum.

filling up sandbags at the bank... So I got a bit of money. Finally, I got myself a job in the East End fitting sewing machines for a firm that fitted sewing machines for people to make khaki uniforms. I got a job there which I enjoyed very much and I got myself a furnished room... It was a Jewish company. He came from Russia. He was a very nice man and did help me. He did realise that I was a refugee boy and things like that. He even got me a permit to work because this was almost war work, setting up machines for war work.[11]

Another unique hardship stood in the way of women who came on domestic visas. The great majority of them were categorized as A or B, and were either interned or restricted, thereby losing their jobs. Moreover, in many cases they were treated badly as servants, and had sometimes to be separated from their families. In many cases they were the only breadwinners and had to support their unemployed husbands.[12]

However, as much as the war put these kinds of hardships in the refugees' way to integration, once the internees were released the war presented economic demands, and when the army opened its gates for refugee enlistment, a new avenue opened. Many of the internees, once released, joined the army, many others found jobs in the war economy. Both in the army and at home they now became much more integrated, economically and socially.

Figure 21: Group portrait of the X Troop – a unit of German speaking British soliders, officially the 3rd Troop of the Tenth Inter-Allied IA Commandos, circa 1943 – 1944. Courtesy of the U.S. Holocaust memorial Museum.

---

11 Interview with Willy Field (Hirschfeld), 17 June, 2003, WLL, Refugee Voices 21.
12 Kushner (1991).

German-Jewish Presence in Britain

The 83,000 German-speaking Jews who reached the British shores after the rise of Hitler to power were actually the only Jews immigrating to Britain in those years. Their substantial number accounted for 28 percent of the 300,000 Jews already residing in the country. Even if we consider only the 45,000 to 50,000 who remained in Britain, we get a significant proportion of 17 percent.

The immigrants to Britain concentrated mainly in London, where they gathered in the north-west communities of Hampstead, Belsize Park and their vicinity. In those neighborhoods they had their own shops and bakeries, their own restaurants and coffee shops, creating and preserving an isolated island of German-Jewish social and cultural environment, detached from the general environment of their host country.[13]

The impact of the earlier newcomers, though, was quite visible in England, especially in the world of arts, theater, music and publishing, in which they introduced the up-to-date modern approaches developed in Weimar Berlin and interwar Vienna.[14] There are also a few studies showing the instrumental role of German-Jewish industrialists on underdeveloped regions, especially in Northern England, and on innovations in new products and marketing methods especially in textiles, fur and leather industries.[15]

In the Jewish sphere the German immigrants were also quite visible. Teachers came to Britain and in some cases participated in the process of absorption of young refugees by establishing their own schools, as was the case in London.[16] These schools existed, however, only for a transitional period. Famous rabbis, among them Leo Baeck, the liberal leader of German Jewry, founded their congregations in Britain. In some instances whole congregations with their religious functionaries immigrated to England and established there upon arrival a replica of their former congregations. Many German-Jewish congregations were thus established in England, joining the various existing trends – Liberal, Reform, Orthodox and Ultra-Orthodox.[17]

---

13 Grenville (1999, 2002).
14 Berghaus (1989); Snowman (2002).
15 AJR Information, May 1946; Berghahn (1984); Gelber (1990); Loebl (1991); Pollins (1991).
16 Testimonies by Charles Hofner and Elly Miller to the author, London 2007, Personal Collection.
17 Homa (1969); Kershen and Romain (1995); Maybaum (1951).

"Continental Britons": Self-Perception and Organization

Britain was scarcely prepared for the new task of absorbing immigrants on a large scale, and was dominated by anti-alien traditions that made it unreceptive for newcomers.[18] The new, post-1938 immigrants saw themselves, as well as they were considered by others, as refugees, depending on the good will of the British and Jewish authorities. Given their awkward position as German aliens, who turned after the outbreak of the war into enemy aliens, the newcomers had to disguise their identity and refrain from attracting any attention. Consequently, British Jews had to organize their aid facilities against an unwelcoming atmosphere of governmental pressure (permitting only temporary asylum) and hostility.

The first organizational aid initiative was the Jewish Refugee Committee, as mentioned earlier. In 1938, the term "refugees" was omitted and it was renamed German-Jewish Aid Committee. But then again in 1939, to avoid the term "German," the initial name was reinstalled. This flip-flop was just one of many instances demonstrating the insecurity of British Jews and their reservations concerning the new German-Jewish arrivals.

All the Jewish institutions founded to assist Jewish refugees from Germany – and particularly the Council for German Jewry – made huge efforts to enable the refugees – even after they had arrived in the U.K. – to continue on their way and leave Britain. Indeed, they were obliged to follow their commitment to the government to make sure that the provisional entry would not become permanent settlement. Thus, they constantly surveyed how many people did actually leave, as a measurement of success.[19]

The refugees themselves, always confronted with being considered non-British (not to mention the experience of detention and deportation after the outbreak of war), internalized their identity as unwelcome refugees, keeping this sense until the present. They remained forever identified by their German language and culture, and they never fully integrated into the Jewish society in Britain.[20] As a result of the refugees' insecurity, the Association of Jewish Refugees (AJR) was founded only toward the end of the war, its name of course omitting any reference to their origin. Its publication, starting to appear only in 1946, was naturally in

---

18 Laqueur (2001).

19 Sources for facts, not the interpretation: Zahl-Gottlieb (1998); CBF sources – addresses and budgets, WLL; Council for German Jewry sources, WLL; JRC sources, WLL. For an alternative interpretation of England as focus for helping, see Grenville (1999).

20 Grenville (1999, 2002); Laqueur (2001). This feeling of being "refugees" forever was clearly expressed in a series of interviews screened at the exhibition "Continental Britons" at the Jewish Museum in London, 2002.

English only, and its main objective was to follow and promote the process of full integration into English and the English-Jewish society. [21]

The literature about the Jewish interwar immigration from Germany to Britain focuses mainly on the contribution of this immigration to the British economy and culture. Many studies relate also to issues concerning the British immigration policy with divergent evaluations, but stressing that the bottom line is that Britain did much more than other countries to absorb refugees. However, the immigration experience stayed with the immigrants as a decisive factor in their identity as a separate sector in the U.K., "Continental Britons."

---

21 AJR (1951); AJR Information no. 1, 1946.

Conclusion

A Comparative Analysis of Three Immigration Stories

German-Jewish immigration to the major overseas destinations, Palestine, the United States and Britain, varied in terms of demographic, occupational and economic composition as well as in the timing and dynamics of their migration. All of these factors were closely linked. During the 1920s, both Palestine and the United States served as destinations for migrating German Jews, while Britain experienced hardly any German Jewish immigration. The Jews immigrating to the United States were different from those who chose to go to Palestine. America attracted mainly German-Jewish small or medium-sized businessmen, while Palestine was the goal of young professionals and academics, mainly in the early stages of building their careers.

During the Nazi era, despite the common grounds for emigration, different groups of German Jews varied in the timing of their decision to emigrate, and accordingly their options to choose a destination changed. Those who made a quick decision to emigrate were mainly young professionals whose prospect in Germany was dim. For the most part, they chose Palestine as their destination with the exception of high-level academics (both young and old) for whom special arrangements were made in both Britain and the United States. The great majority of German Jews who were driven to emigrate only after the *Kristallnacht* pogrom reflected more or less the average profile of aging German Jewish population, and may be defined as refugees, who were unable anymore to calculate timing or destination and who had extremely limited prospects for transferring what was left of their capital. These were accepted mainly in the United States and in Britain, who responded to the events in Germany by loosening their rigid immigration regulations. Palestine at that time became increasingly closed, particularly following the Arab Revolt of 1936 and the Mandate White Paper of 1939, which severely restricted Jewish immigration in general. Despite the fact that the Mandate government acted more permissively toward immigrants from Germany, Palestine accepted now the smallest share of German-Jewish immigration.

The outcome of these developments was decisive in shaping the different profile of each of the immigrant groups.

It may be difficult to define with any precision the profile of the immigrants to the United States and Britain. While the estimates for Germany and Palestine apply exclusively to Jews, those for the United States and Britain do not distinguish between Jews and non-Jews. Academics and artists who immigrated to those countries included a significant number of non-Jewish political exiles. Our conclusions will therefore be tentative. However, since many if not most immigrants from Germany were Jews or of Jewish descent, it seems reasonable to apply the estimates in a broad sense to the Jews as a migrant and refugee population. It would appear that the group that went to Palestine was relatively young, with considerable means and with skills that helped them to fit into the local economy. German Jews constituted a substantial part of the total Jewish immigration to Palestine at the time and caused the German-speaking element in the country to become much more visible. The group that immigrated to the United States was less homogeneous in terms of age, capital and skills. They included some stellar personalities and Nobel Prize laureates in the arts and sciences, though as time progressed, this influx was more middle- and lower-middleclass, representing the profile of German Jewry in general. The German Jews who immigrated to Britain came at about the same time as many Austrian and Czech Jews. Most of the immigrants came in the late 1930s, and with no possessions, though among them (as in the American case) was a small but visible group of artists and academics, many of them of Viennese origin.

In absolute terms, as well as in its proportional share of the total immigration from Germany over the entire Nazi period, the United States took in more immigrants than did Britain or Palestine. The latter two received similar numbers (45,000 and 53,000 respectively), together (98,000) accounting for about 20 percent more than the number of immigrants to the United States, 82,000. However, these proportions must be seen against the circumstances of each of the countries. Palestinian Jews had already acquired official status as a national community under the British Mandate, and Jewish immigration was a central and dominant aspect of its life and development. The German Jews immigrating to Palestine comprised more than 20 percent of the immigration wave of the 1930s, which doubled the size of the *Yishuv*. They differed socially and culturally in the context of their new home, but it may be said that Central European immigrants of the 1920s and 1930s provided Jewish Palestine with a much-needed modernizing cohort. The immigrants to the United States and Britain must likewise be viewed against the general background in these countries, and in particular against the background of their Jewish communities. It may well be assumed that Central European Jews (including Germans, Austrians and Czechs) constituted the majority of the European immigration to the United States at the time. What bears remembering as well was that, unlike the case of Palestine, there was a significant Central European descent group among American Jewry, established over the course of the previous century. Representative figures of German-American Jewry still maintained their hegemonic position after World War I and through much of the 1930s. Given this background a reasonable conjecture is that the latter-day immigration from Nazi Germany had very little qualitative or differentiating impact on the established Jewish community. To the contrary perhaps, the American-Jewish elite of German origin felt more sympathy towards German-Jewish refugees or the refugees might have felt more comfortable with the German-Jewish American establishment, but our study did not reveal any evidence supporting this assumption.

In some ways, the Central European Jewish immigration of the 1930s was as significant for British Jewry as it was for Palestine. In both countries, this influx brought a new cultural element into the existing mix of Eastern European and Sephardic Jewry. In Britain, though, it is hard to distinguish the Germans from the Austrians and the Czechs, who made up about one third of the refugee migration. Thus, whereas for Palestine estimation of the German-Jewish component is of 22 percent (and together with other Central Europeans, 25 percent) of the total Jewish immigration of that time, the 83,000 German-speaking Jews who reached British shores after 1933 actually comprised the entire Jewish immigration to Britain in this period, and accounted for an increase of 28 percent in the Anglo-Jewish population (this figure drops to 17 percent if only net immigration is considered). In the United States, it may be recalled, the influx of German-speaking immigrants during the Nazi era added only slightly more than 3 percent to the total Jewish population.

Britain, like Palestine, experienced the presence of many German Jews as an unprecedented challenge. But contrary to Palestine, Britain and its Jewish community were far less prepared for absorbing the newcomers, and the fortunes of the refugees were dominated by an anti-alien tradition.

In Palestine, the immigrants were assisted by their predecessors and by the machinery created by the Zionist Organization and Jewish welfare institutions. They quickly formed a *Landsmannschaft*, and also a political party that got involved in the politics of the Jewish national home – not in order to advance narrow sectorial interests, but rather those values deemed of particular importance to the national Zionist project. Political activism of that sort was not possible in the United States or in Britain, where even the most effectively integrated could not exert any palpable public influence.

Even ignoring the political dimension, the Palestinian case was unique in terms of the immigrants' high level of self-confidence. The British case displays the extreme opposite situation, where the mistrust of the general public and the lack of confidence among the established Jewish community prompted a low-profile policy.

It might also be noted that the extent to which German Jewish immigrants tended to live separately from other Jews was highest in the British case.

Common sense, or intuition, leads to the assumption that in the encounter of the immigrants with their new host societies they found that they as immigrants had much in common, given their common German heritage, social and economic fabric, and education. In all three countries, the immigrants suffered from losing their former social and economic status. In all three cases they tenaciously worked their way up the economic and social ladder, and the role of women in this process was decisive. Despite initial difficulties they did not give up their aspirations for cultural consumption at a high level. As for the encounter with the local Jewish community, in all three cases it was marked by mutual frictions that hampered complete social integration. However, it seems that the differences between the receiving countries were much more decisive than the common features, with Palestine and Britain representing two extremes along a continuum and the United States positioned somewhere in between.

Although the immigrants to Palestine experienced a drop in their standard of living, it is likely to have been less difficult for them compared with the loss of social status experienced by those immigrating to the United States or Britain. This assumption is based on four factors. First, immigrants to Palestine usually did not come from among the most prosperous echelons of German Jewish society, whereas many of those who went to Britain and the United States came precisely from among the most integrated and partially from the most affluent German Jewish circles. Second, many of those who immigrated to the United States and Britain did so quite late, when they were prohibited from taking much or any of their possessions. The majority of the immigrants to Palestine, in contrast, came early enough, and under a more permissive emigration regime, to enable them to bring along a considerable part of their capital. Third, many of the newcomers to Palestine could apply their skills and professions, for which there was a demand, almost immediately, so that they experienced a relatively minor amount of status dislocation. And fourth, the Palestinian Jewish middle class was much less prosperous, on average, than its counterparts in the United States and Britain. Therefore, the new immigrants did not suffer from relative deprivation as measured by local criteria.

It seems that the effort to rebuild a solid existence, not to speak of moving up economically, academically or occupationally, was much harder in the United States and Britain than in Palestine, where the economic integration of the immigrants was rapid, and where their impact on various economic and cultural sectors was recognized and appreciated.

At the same time, those who came to Palestine experienced significant culture shock, encountering a Jewish society whose Middle Eastern and Eastern European components alike appeared to be "inferior" to their own culture, and in addition was situated as a minority group in the Orient and under the impact of a problematic relationship with the Arab majority population. Encountering this situation produced impending social and political challenges of integration. In comparison, immigrants to the United States and Britain were ostensibly "cushioned" by a more familiar, Western social and cultural environment. The cultural issue in Palestine may have been offset somewhat by the comparative economic advantage of the immigrants, but may also have added a special impetus to their unique organizational behavior.

The German immigrants revolutionized the Palestinian economy. The high proportion of industrialists and the diversity of new branches they established helped to modernize the infant Palestinian Jewish industry. In Britain, the impact was limited to less developed regions of the country. The proportion of agricultural workers in Jewish Palestine was the largest of any Jewish community, and the German-Jewish impact in this field was also unparalleled among the receiving countries. The transfer of German-Jewish medical and social services had a profound impact in Palestine, whereas many of the physicians who immigrated to the United States or Britain were confronted with restrictions that delayed or blocked their professional reintegration.

The top German-Jewish scientists went to the United States or Britain, which offered not only attractive academic environments but also created special mechanisms to facilitate the migration and absorption process. Palestine's academic infrastructure, in contrast, was still in its infancy, and no special incentives were available to the new immigrants. However, though both the United States and Britain gained substantially from German immigrant scientists, this input was only an addition, albeit qualitatively significant, to an existing and well-developed infrastructure. In Palestine, the immigrants who came with academic credentials quite literally changed their new land. Moreover, this change had a Jewish-cultural aspect. The intellectual transfer to the United States and Britain was universal in character, possessing little, if any, specific Jewish dimension. In contrast, the transfer to Palestine was evident, first of all, in the field of Jewish studies, which had developed as a modern academic endeavor in the German context.

Among the immigrants to Palestine there was a high percentage of teachers who had a distinct and lasting impact on Jewish education in general, both secular and religious. In the realm of the arts, the picture is different – here, the United States and Britain derived more benefit from immigrant artists and performers. In certain fields, such as the film industry, the German-Austrian immigration to the United States was of crucial importance. In other fields, such as music and publishing, Britain experienced a revolution as a result of the immigration. Palestine, although influenced by immigrant artistic creators and producers the most decisive factors in this realm was the implementation of new standards and concepts of cultural demand and consumption or, in other words, the Westernization and modernization of the local cultural attitudes and standards.

Pondering the question which German-Jewish Diaspora succeeded most in integration and "disappearing" within the general society, the answer would be – the United States, where the immigrants and their following generation do not manifest much self-awareness of their origins and there was little if any visible effort to emphasize or to foster exposition of the German-Jewish element as a unique component within the American pluralistic social fabric, except for a very limited circle of intellectuals who contemplate their German legacy.

In Palestine and Britain the immigrants largely preserved their self-awareness as a cultural community, but the difference between the two was in their perception of their experiences as immigrants. While in Britain the dominant perception was of understanding themselves as thankful refugees, in Palestine they nurtured the perception of proud immigrants who contributed decisively to the local society.

But if posing the question of which branch succeeded best in implementing its German-Jewish legacy, the answer would be Palestine/Israel. This is manifested by the ways in which each of these two groups of immigrants – to Britain and to Palestine/Israel – remembers and memorializes its immigration experience, whereas the American group is undoubtedly the most successfully integrated and socially dispersed.

Sources and Bibliography

Archives

AJR = Association of Jewish Refugees: http://www.ajr.org.uk

CZA = Central Zionist Archives, Jerusalem
The Central Bureau for the Settlement of German Jews in Palestine (S7).
JA Immigration Department (S4).
JA Political Department (S25).

IWM = Imperial War Museum, London
Sound Archives.

LBIANY = Leo Baeck Institute Archives, New York
Salomon Adler-Rudel Collection (AR 4473).
American Federation of Jews from Central Europe (AR 4420; AR 126).
German-Jewish Club of 1933 (AR 6466).
L. Grebler (1976) *German-Jewish immigrants to the United States during the Hitler period*
(Unpublished manuscript, ME 716).
Memoires Collection.

NARA = National Archives and Record Administration, USA
The World War II Army Enlistment Records and database (RG 59).

OHD = the Oral History Division, the Institute of Contemporary Jewry, the Hebrew University of Jerusalem
Project no. 183 · Interviews conducted by the author in 1982.

USHMM = United States Holocaust Memorial Museum Archives
Interviews Collection.
Private Archives/Collections.
Survivors Testimonies and Memoirs.

WLL = Wiener Library London
Central British Fund (CBF) Collection.
Refugee Voices: The AJR Audio-Visual Testimony Archive.

YIVO Archives
Academic Assistance Council Annual Reports.
Joseph Perkins Chamberlain Collection (RG 278).
HIAS material (RG 245).
Joint Reports = American Jewish Joint Distribution Committee Reports (printed).
The Records of the National Refugee Service 1934–1952 (RG 248).

Irgun Yots'ei Merkaz Eropa: http://www.irgun-jeckes.org

Periodicals

AJR Information Bulletin: http://www.ajr.org.uk
Aufbau: http://deposit.ddb.de/online/exil/exil.htmhttp://archive.org/stream/
     aufbau1519341939germ#page/n0/mode/1up

Personal Collection of the Author

Lotte Hamburger interview, Washington, D.C., 2005
Charles Hofner (of blessed memory) and Elly Miller to the author, London, 2007.
Shmuel Kneller lecture on 9 November, 2008, Haifa
Mathias Marburg (2000) HOG und *Landsmanschaften* (seminar paper).
Martin and Eva Plessner testimonies, Jerusalem
Viola Rautenberg-Alianov (2013),'"I don't know if you can understand what it means to be on
     the outside like this...". Letters of German-Jewish Immigrants to the "German Department"
     and the HOG in the 1930s, presented at the Inter-University Forum for the Study of
     Migration, the University of Haifa, 24 November, 2013.

Publications Cited

R. Adler (2012) Immigration Act of 1924, http://immigrationinamerica.org/590-immigration-act-
     of-1924.html (last entry 8 April, 2015).
AJR (1951) *Britain's New Citizens. The Story of the Refugees from Germany and Austria 1941–1951*
     (10th anniversary of AJR), London: Association of Jewish Refugees in Great Britain.
G. Alroey (1993) "'Ruslan': Ha'umnam Hasenunit Harishona Hamevasseret et Bo Ha'aliya
     Hashelishit?," *Katedra* 107: 63–80.
G. Alroey (2002) "Haherkev Hademografi shel Ha'aliya Hasheniya," *Israel* 2: 33–55.
G. Alroey (2004) *Immigrantim: Hahagira Hayehudit Le'eretz Israel Bereshit Hame'a Ha'esrim*,
     Jerusalem: Yad Ben-Zvi Press.
G. Alroey (2007) *Hamahapekha Hasheketa: Hahagirah Hayehudit Mehaimperia Harussit
     1875–1924*, Jerusalem: Zalman Shazar Center for Jewish History.
M.M. Anderson (1998) *Hitler's Exiles: Personal Stories of the Flight from Nazi Germany to
     America*, New York: The New Press.
N. Angell and D.F. Buxton (1939) *You and the Refugee: The Morals and Economics of
     the Problem; The Truth about Unemployment, Immigration, and Depopulation*,
     Harmondsworth, Middlesex, Eng: Penguin Books Limited.
S.E. Aschheim (2007) *Beyond the Border: The German-Jewish Legacy Abroad*, Princeton and
     Oxford: Princeton University Press.
R. Bachi (1974) *The Population of Israel*, Jerusalem: Scientific Translation International.
E. Bahr (2007) *Weimar on the Pacific: German Exile Culture in Los Angeles and the Crisis of
     Modernism*, Berkeley: University of California Press.

S.L. Baily (1999) *Immigrants in the Lands of Promise: Italians in Buenos Aires and New York City, 1870–1914*, Ithaca and London: Cornell University Press.

K.J. Ball-Kaduri (1967) *Vor der Katastrophe: Juden in Deutschland, 1934–1939*, Tel Aviv: Olamenu.

A. Barkai (1989) *From Boycott to Annihilation: The Economic Struggle of German Jews, 1933–1943*, Hanover, NH: University Press of New England.

A. Barkai (1994) *Branching Out: German-Jewish Immigration to the United States, 1820–1914*, New York and London: Holmes & Meier.

A. Barkai (1997) "Bevölkerungsrückgang und wirtschaftliche Stagnation," in: Avraham Barkai and Paul Mendes-Flohr, *Aufbruch und Zerstörubg 1918–1945* (*Deutsch-jüdische Geschichte in der Neuzeit*, Band IV, gen. ed. Michael A. Meyer), Munich: C. H. Beck, 37–49.

A. Barkai and P. Mendes-Flohr (1997) *Aufbruch und Zerstörubg 1918–1945* (*Deutsch-jüdische Geschichte in der Neuzeit*, Band IV, gen. ed. Michael A. Meyer), Munich: C. H. Beck.

S. Barron and S. Eckmann (1997) *Exiles+Emigres: The Flight of European Artists from Hitler* (CA County Museum of Art, Catalog of Exhibition), Los Angeles: Los Angeles County Museum of Art.

A. Bein (1992) *Kan ein Mevarkhim Leshalom: Zikhronot*, Jerusalem: Bialik Institute.

E. Beling (1967) *Die gesellschaftliche Eingliederung der deutschen Einwanderer in Israel*, Frankfurt a/M: Europäische Verlagsanstalt.

A. Benari (1986) *Zikhronot shel Halutz me-Eretz Ashkenaz*, Hazore'a: Hazore'a.

S. Ben-Chorin (1974) *Jugend an der Isar*, Munich: List Verlag.

N. Bentwich (1936) *The Refugees from Germany, April 1933 to December 1935*, London: G. Allen & Unwin, ltd.

W. Benz (1991) *Das Exil der kleinen Leute: Alltagserfahrung deutscher Juden in der Emigration*, München: C.H. Beck.

W. Benz (1998) "Die jüdische Emigration," in: *Handbuch der deutschsprachigen Emigration 1933–1945*, Claus-Dieter Krohn, Elisabeth Kohlhaas in Zusammenarbeit mit der Gesellschaft für Exilforschung (eds.), Darmstadt: Primus Verlag, 5–15.

M. Berghahn (1984) *German-Jewish Refugees in England: The Ambiguities of Assimilation*, New York: St. Martin's Press.

G. Berghaus (1989) *Theatre and Film in Exile: German Artists in Britain, 1933–1945*, Oxford: Berg.

A. Betten and M. Du-nour (2000) *Sprachbewahrung nach der Emigration – Das Deutsch der 20er Jahre in Israel* (PHONAI, Bd. 45), Tübingen: Max Niemeyer Verlag.

H. Bickelman (1980) *Deutsche Überseeauswanderung in der Weimarer Zeit*, Wiesbaden: F. Steiner.

B. Blau (1950) *Die Entwicklung der jüdischen Bevölkerung in Deutschland von 1800–1940*, New York: s. n.

R. Boehling and U. Larkey (2011) *Life and Loss in the Shadow of the Holocaust: A Jewish Family's Untold Story*, Cambridge: Cambridge University Press.

R. Bondy (1990) *Felix: Pinhas Rosen Uzemano*, Tel Aviv: Zmora-Bitan.

R. Breitman and A.M. Kraut (1987) *American Refugee Policy and European Jewry 1933–1945*, Bloomington: Indiana University Press.

R. Breitman et al. (2009) *Refugees and Rescue: The Diaries and Papers of James G. McDonald, 1935–1945*, Bloomington: Indiana University Press.

T. Brinkmann (2010) "Jewish Migration," http://ieg-ego.eu/en/threads/europe-on-the-road/jewish-migration#19141948ExpulsionShoahandthefoundationofIsrael (last accessed, 10 April, 2015).

R. Brinkmann and C. Wolff (1999) *Driven into Paradise: The Musical Migration from Nazi Germany to the United States*, Berkeley: University of California Press.

I. Britschgi-Schimmer (1936) *Die Umschichtung der jüdischen Einwanderer aus Deutschland zu städtischen Berufen in Palästina,* Jerusalem: The Jewish Agency, Central Bureau for the Settlement of German Jews in Palestine.

W. Cohn (2014) *Betsipornei Haraykh Hashelishi: Yomano shel Willy Cohn 1933–1941*, translated from the German manuscript by Avraham (Ernst) Cohn ed. Tamar Gazit, Jerusalem: The Hebrew University Magnes Press.

L.A. Coser (1984) *Refugee Scholars in America: Their Impact and Their Experience*, New Haven: Yale University Press.

U. Dagan (2011) *Kibbutz Ga'aguim*, Tel Aviv: Gevanim.

R. Daniels (1986) "Changes in immigration law and nativism since 1924," *Jewish History*, 76: 159–180.

J. Davidson (1991) "German-Jewish Women in England," in: Werner Mosse (ed.), *Second Chance: Two Centuries of German-Speaking Jews in the United Kingdom*, Tübingen: J.C.B. Mohr P. Siebeck, 533–551.

M.R. Davie (1947) *Refugees in America: Report of the Committee for the Study of Recent Immigration from Europe*, New York, London: Harper & Bros.

M.R. Davie and S. Koenig (1945) *The Refugees are now Americans*, New York: Public Affairs Committee, inc.

A.Y. Deter (2004) "Introduction," in: *Lives Lost, Lives Found: Baltimore German Jewish Refugees 1933–1945*, Baltimore, Md.: Jewish Museum of Maryland.

Deutsche Alijah (1935) *Die deutsche Alijah in der Histadruth (ein Bericht über das Landestreffen Tel Aviv, 25.-27. April 1935)*, Tel Aviv: Achdut.

H.R. Diner (1992) *A Time for Gathering: The Second Migration, 1820–1880 (The Jewish People in America,* ed. Henry L. Feingold, vol. 2), Baltimore: Johns Hopkins University Press.

S.N. Eisenstadt (1954) "Aliya Vahagirah," *Metsuda*, vol. VII: 83–91.

C. Epstein (1993) *A Past Renewed: A Catalogue of German-Speaking Refugee Historians in the U.S. after 1933*, Cambridge: Cambridge University Press.

H.L. Feingold (1992) *A Time for Searching: Entering the Mainstream, 1920–1945 (The Jewish People in America,* ed. Henry L. Feingold, vol. 4), Baltimore: Johns Hopkins University Press.

H. Fields (1938) *The Refugee in the United States*, New York: Oxford University Press.

D. Fraenkel (1994) *Al Pi Tehom: Hamediniyut Hatsiyonit Ushe'elat Yehudei Germanya 1933–1938*, Jerusalem: The Hebrew University Magnes Press.

S. Friedländer (1997) *Nazi Germany and the Jews*, vol. I: *The Years of Persecution, 1933–1939*, New York: HarperCollins.

L. Garland (2014) *After They Closed the Gates: Jewish Illegal Immigration to the United States, 1921–1965*, Chicago and London: University of Chicago Press.

L. Gartner (1960) *The Jewish Immigration in England 1870–1914*, London: Allen & Unwin.

L.P. Gartner (1998) "The Great Jewish Immigration: Its East-European Background," *Tel Aviver Jahrbuch für Geschichte*, vol. XXVII: 107–136.

Y.G. Gelber (1987) "Deutsche Juden in Politischen Leben des Jüdischen Palästina, 1933–1948," *Leo Baeck Institute Bulletin*, 76: 51–72.

Y. Gelber (1990) *Moledet Hadasha: Aliyat Yehudei Merkaz Eropa Ukelitatam, 1933–1948*, Jerusalem: Yad Ben-Zvi Press.

M. Getter (1979) "Ha'aliya Migermania Bashanim 1933–1939," *Cathedra* 12: 125–147.

M. Getter (1982) "Hahit'argenut hapolitit hanifredet shel olei germanya," *Hatsiyonut* 7, 240–191

Goldfein (1993) *Ha'aliya Hahamishit: 60 Shana La'aliya Mimerkaz Eropa (Katalog Ta'arukha)*, Tel Aviv: Irgun Olei Merkaz Eropa.

A. Golz (2009) *Refuat Af-Ozen-Garon Be'eretz Israel 1911–1948*, Zikhron Yaacov: Itay Bahur Publishing.

A. Golz (2013) *Batei Holim Peratiyim Be'eretz Israel*, Zikhron Yaakov: Itay Bahur Publishing.

A. Gordon (2004) '*Bepalestina. Banekhar.*' Jerusalem: The Hebrew University Magnes Press.

G. Greif et al. (2000) *Die Jekkes. Deutsche Juden aus Israel erzählen*, Köln/ Weimar/ Wien: Böhlau.

A. Grenville (1999) "The Integration of Aliens: The Early Years of the Association of Jewish Refugees Information, 1946–1950," *Yearbook of the Research Centre for German and Austrian Exiles Studies*, vol. 1, *German-Speaking Exiles in Great Britain*, ed. Ian Wallace, Amsterdam: 1–23.

A. Grenville (2002) *Continental Britons. Jewish Refugees from Nazi Europe*, London: The Association of Jewish Refugees and the Jewish Museum.

N.T. Gross (1999) "Kelitat Olim Akadema'im Bishenot Ha'esrim Vehamehkar hahidrologi," in: Nahum T. Gross, *Lo al Haruah Levada: Iyunim Bahistorya Hakalkalit shel Eretz-Yisra'el Ba'et Hahadasha*, Jerusalem: The Hebrew University Magnes Press, 273–286.

D. Hacohen (2011) *Yaldei Hazeman: Aliyat HaNo'ar 1933–1948*, Jerusalem: Yad Vashem International Institute for Holocaust Research.

H. Hagemann and C.D. Krohn (1999) *Biographisches Handbuch der deutschsprachigen wirtschaftswissenschaftlichen Emigration nach 1933* (2 vols.), Munich: K.G. Saur.

A. Halamish (2006) *Bemeruts Kaful neged Hazeman: Mediniyut Ha'aliya Ha'tsiyonit Bishenot Hasheloshim*, Jerusalem: Yad Ben-Zvi Press.

M. Hassler and J. Wertheimer (1997) *Der Exodus aus Nazideutschland und die Folgen: Jüdische Wissenschaftler im Exil*, Tübingen: Attempto.

A. Heilbut (1997) *Exiled in Paradise: German Refugee Artists and Intellectuals in America from the 1930s to the Present*, Berkeley: University of California Press.

A. Helman (2007) *Or Veyam Hekifuha: Tarbut Tel Avivit Betekufat Hamandat*, Haifa: University of Haifa Press.

U.D. Herscher (1982) *The East-European Jewish Experience in America: A Century of Memories 1882–1982*, Cincinnati: American Jewish Archives.

J. Hirsch and E. Hirsch (1961) "Berufliche Eingliederung und wirtschaftliche Leistung der deutsch-juedischen Einwanderung in die Vereinigten Staaten (1935–1960)," in: *Twenty years American Federation of Jews from Central Europe, 1940–1960*, New York: American Federation of Jews from Central Europe, 41–70.

E.E. Hirshler (1955) "Jews from Germany in the United States," in: Eric E. Hirshler (ed.), *Jews from Germany in the United States*, New York: Farrar, 89–100.

C. Holmes (1991) *A Tolerant Country? Immigrants, Refugees and Minorities in Britain*, London and Boston: Faber and Faber.

B. Homa (1969) *Orthodoxy in Anglo-Jewry, 1880–1940*, London: Jewish Historical Society of England.

J-C. Horak (1986) *Fluchtpunkt Hollywood: eine Dokumentation zur Filmemigration nach 1933*, Münster: MAkS Publikationen.

S.H. Hughes (1975) *The Sea Change: The Migration of Social Thought, 1930–1965*, New York: Harper & Row.

JA (1939) *Report of the executives of the Zionist organisation and of the Jewish Agency for Palestine, submitted to the 21 Zionist Congress and the 6 session of the Council of the*

Jewish Agency at Geneva, Elul, 5699, August, 1939, Jerusalem: The Executives of the Zionist Organisation and of the Jewish Agency for Palestine.

M.J. Jay (1986) *Permanent Exiles: Essays on the Intellectual Migration from Germany to America*, New York: Columbia University Press.

M. Jay (1997) "The German Migration: Is There a Figure in the Carpet?" in: Stephanie Barron, Matthew Affron, Sabine Eckmann, Los Angeles County Museum of Art, Montreal Museum of Fine Arts, Neue Nationalgalerie Germany (eds.), *Exiles + Emigrés: The Flight of European Artists from Hitler*, Los Angeles: Los Angeles County Museum of Art, 320–326.

D.P. Kent (1953) *The Refugee Intellectual: The Americanization of the Immigrants of 1933–1941*, New York: Columbia University Press.

A.J. Kershen and J.A. Romain (1995) *Tradition and Change: A History of Reform Judaism in Britain 1840–1995*, London: Vallentine, Mitchell.

R. Kobrin (2010) *Jewish Bialystok and Its Diaspora*, Bloomington and Indianapolis: Indiana University Press.

J. Kocka (2003) "Comparison and Beyond," *History and Theory* 42: 39–44.

C.D. Krohn (1993) *Intellectuals in Exile: Refugee Scholars and the New School for Social Research*, Amherst, Mass: University of Massachusetts Press.

C.D. Krohn (1998) "Die Vereinigten Staaten," in: Claus-Dieter Krohn, Elisabeth Kohlhaas, Gesellschaft für Exilforschung, *Handbuch der deutschsprachigen Emigration, 1933–1945*, Darmstadt: Primus Verlag, 446–466.

T. Kushner (1991) "An Alien Occupation – Jewish Refugees and Domestic Service in Britain 1933–1948," in: Werner Mosse (ed.), *Second Chance: Two Centuries of German-Speaking Jews in the United Kingdom*, Tübingen: J.C.B. Mohr P. Siebeck, 553–578.

W. Laqueur (2001) *Generation Exodus: The Fate of Young Jewish Refugees from Nazi Germany*, Hanover, NH: Brandeis University Press.

H. Lavsky (1987) "The German Inflation and the Crises Afterwards (1922–1926) from a Zionist Point of View," *Hatsiyonut*, XII: 165–181.

H. Lavsky (1996) *Before Catastrophe: The Distinctive Path of German Zionism*, Detroit: Wayne State University Press; Jerusalem: Magnes Press, Leo Baeck Institute.

H. Lavsky (2003) "Le'umiyut, Hagira Vehityashvut: Ha'im Hayta Mediniyut Kelita Tsionit?" in: Avi Bareli and Nahum Karlinsky (eds.), *Kalkala Vehevra Biyemei Hamandat 1918–1948* (Iyunim Bitkumat Israel, Tematic Series 2) Sede Boqer: The Ben-Gurion Research Institute, Ben-Gurion University of the Negev, 153–177.

H. Lavsky (2009) "Madua Ne'edra Yahadut Germanya Mishurat Hamanhigim Batsiyonut Ubayishuv?"*Divrei Hakongress Ha'olami Hahamisha-assar Lemadaei Hayahadut*, http://www.jewish-studies.org/ShowDoc.asp?MenuID=63.

H. Lavsky (2014) "Me'aliya Hadasha Lamiflaga Haperogresivit," in: Mordechai Bar-On and Meir Hazan (eds.), *Ha'ezrahim Bemilhemet Ha'atsma'ut, 3: Politika Bemilhama*, Jerusalem: Yad Ben-Zvi Press, 322–343.

H. Lehmann (1991) *An Interrupted Past. German Speaking Refugee Historians in the United States after 1933*, Washington, D.C.: German Historical Institute.

J. Lestschinsky (1944) *Jewish Migration for the Past Hundred Years*, New York, N.Y: Yiddish Scientific Institute YIVO, 1944.

J. Lestschinsky (1965) *Nedudei Yisra'el Badorot Ha'aharonim*, Tel Aviv: Aleph.

A. Levy (2016) "A Man of Contention: Martin Plessner (1900–1973) and his Encounters with the Orient," *Naharaim*, 10, 1: 79–100.

R. Lichtheim (1951) *Toldot Hatsiyonut Begermanya*, Jerusalem: Hasifriya Hatsiyonit.

H.S. Linfield (1933) *Jewish Migration: Jewish Migration as a Part of World Migration Movements, 1920–1930*, New York: Jewish Statistical Bureau.

Lives Lost (2004) *Lives Lost, Lives Found: Baltimore German Jewish Refugees, 1933–1945* (Exhibition Catalog), Baltimore: The Jewish Museum of Maryland.

H. Loebl (1983) "Flüchtlingsunternehmen in den wirtschaftlichen Kriesengebieten Grossbritanniens," in: Gerhard Hirschfeld (ed.), *Exil in Grossbritannien: zur Emigration aus dem Nationalsozialistischen Deutschland*, Stuttgart: Klett-Cotta, 205–235.

H. Loebl (1991) "Refugees from the Third Reich and Industry in the Depressed Areas of Britain," in: Werner Mosse (ed.), *Second Chance: Two Centuries of German-Speaking Jews in the United Kingdom*, Tübingen: J.C.B. Mohr P. Siebeck, 379–403.

S.M. Loewenstein (1989) *Frankfurt on the Hudson: The German-Jewish Community of Washington Heights, Its Structure and Culture*, Detroit: Wayne State University Press.

M. Malina (1931) *Deutsche Juden in New York nach dem Weltkriege*, New York [s. n.].

A. Margaliot and Y. Cochavi (1998) *Toldot Hasho'a: Germanya*, Jerusalem: Yad Vashem.

M. Marrus (2002) *The Unwanted: European Refugees in the 20th Century* (with a new Forword by Aristide R. Zolberg), Philadelphia: Temple University Press.

I. Marßolek and W. Davids (1997) *"Man hängt immer zwischen Himmel und Erde…" Jüdische Emigrantinnen und Emigranten (1933–1945) aus Bremen Berichten* (kleine Schriften des Staatsarchivs Bremen, Heft 28), Bremen: Selbstverlag des Staatsarchivs Bremen.

J. Matthäus and M. Roseman (2010) *Jewish Responses to Persecution, vol. I: 1933–1938*, Lanham, MD: AltaMira Press in association with the United States Holocaust Memorial Museum, Washington, D.C.

R.I. Maybaum (1951) "German Jews and Anglo-Jewry," in: Association of Jewish Refugees in Great Britain, *Britain's New Citizens. The Story of the Refugees from Germany and Austria 1941–1951* (10th anniversary of AJR), London: Association of Jewish Refugees in Great Britain.

Y. Mendel (2016) "German Orientalism, Arabic Grammar and the Jewish Education System: The Origins and Effect of Martin Plessner's *Theory of Arabic Grammar*," *Naharaim*, 10, 1: 57–77.

J. Metzer (1998) *The Divided Economy of Mandatory Palestine*, Cambridge: Cambridge University Press.

J. Metzer (2008) "Jewish immigration to Palestine in the long 1920s: An exploratory examination," *The Journal of Israeli History*, 27/2: 221–251.

M.A. Meyer (2001) *Judaism within Modernity: Essays in Jewish History and Religion*, Detroit: Wayne State University Press.

G. Miron (2005) *Mi'sham' Le'khan' Beguf Rishon: Zikhronoteihem shel Yots'ei Germanya Be'yisrael*, Jerusalem: The Koebner Center and the Hebrew University Magnes Press.

W. Mock (1986) *Technische Intelligenz im Exil: Vertreibung und Emigration deutschprachiger Inginieure nach Grossbritannien 1933 bis 1945*, Düsseldorf: VDI Verlag.

M. Mosek (1976) "Herbert Samuel Ve'itzuv Hadefusim shel Mediniyut Ha'aliya," in: Yehuda Bauer, Moshe Davis and Israel Kolatt (eds.), *Pirkei Mehkar Betoldot Hatsiyonut*, Jerusalem: Hasifriya Hatsiyonit and the Institute of Contemporary Jewry, the Hebrew University of Jerusalem, 286–310.

H. Nathorff (1987) *Das Tagebuch der Hertha Nathorff: Berlin-New York, Aufzeichnungen 1933 bis 1945*, herausgegeben und eingeleitet von Wolfgang Benz, Munich:, R. Oldenbourg with the Institut für Zeitgeschichte.

A. Newman and S.W. Massil (1996) *Patterns of migration, 1850–1914: proceedings of the international academic conference of the Jewish Historical Society of England and the*

Institute of Jewish Studies, University College London, London: Jewish Historical Society of England in association with the Institute of Jewish Studies, University College London.

D. Niederland (1983) "Hashpa'at Harof'im Ha'olim Migermanya al Hitpathut Harefua Be'eretz-yisrael (1933–1948)," *Cathedra* 30: 111–160.

D. Niederland (1988) "The Emigration of Jewish Academics and Professionals from Germany in the First Years of Nazi Rule," *Leo Baeck Institute Year Book* 33: 285–300.

D. Niederland (1996) *Yehudei Germanya: Mehagrim O Peltim?*, Jerusalem: The Hebrew University Magnes Press.

D. Niederland (2004) "From Frankfurt to Jerusalem: Horev School. A Special Approach in the Israeli Religious School System," in: Shlomo Berger, Michael Brocke, Irene Zwiep (eds.), *Zutot*, Dordrecht: Springer, 142–152.

G. Ofrat (1987) *Bezalel Hahadash 1935–1955*, Jerusalem: Bezalel Academy of Arts and Design.

A. Oren (1989) "The 'Kfar Shitufi': A New Settlement Type Founded by German Middle-Class Immigrants," in: Ruth Kark (ed.), *The Land that Became Israel*, New Haven: Yale University Press; Jerusalem: Magnes Press, 233–249.

A.J. Peck (1989) *The German-Jewish Legacy in America 1938–1988*, Detroit: Wayne State University Press.

H-D. Petzina (1978) Heinz-Dietmar Petzina, Werner Abelshauser, Anselm Faust, (eds.), *Sozial-geschichtliche Arbeitsbuch III: Materialien zur Statistik des deutschen Reiches, 1914–1945*, Munich: C.H. Beck.

H. Pollins (1991) "German Jews in British Industry," in: Werner Mosse (ed.), *Second Chance: Two Centuries of German-Speaking Jews in the United Kingdom*, Tübingen: J.C.B. Mohr P. Siebeck, 361–377.

Population (1962) *Population and Homes Census 1961: Demographic Characteristics of the Population*, Part II, Jerusalem: Central Bureau of Statistics.

H. Pross (1955) *Die deutsche akademische Emigration nach dem Vereinigten Staaten, 1933–1941*, Berlin: Duncker & Humblot.

S. Quack (1995) "Changing Gender Roles and Emigration: The Example of German-Jewish Women and Their Emigration to the United States, 1933–1945," in Dirk Hoerder and Jörg Nagler (eds.) *People in Transit: German Migrations in Comparative Perspective, 1820–1930*, Cambridge: Cambridge University Press, 379–397.

S. Quack (1995a) *Between Sorrow and Strength: Women Refugees of the Nazi Period*, New York: Cambridge University Press.

Refugee Facts (1939) American Friends Service Committee, *Refugee Facts. A Study of the German Refugee in America*, Philadelphia: America Friends Service Committee.

G. Römer (1987) *Die Austreibung der Juden aus Schwaben. Schicksale nach 1933 in Berichten, Dokumenten, Zahlen und Bildern*, Augsburg: Presse-Druck-und Verlags-GmbH.

E.J. Rolnik (2007) *Osei Hanefashot: Im Froid Le'eretz Yisra'el 1918–1948*, Tel Aviv: Am Oved.

W. Rosenstock (1951) "The Jewish Refugees; Some Facts," in: Association of Jewish Refugees in Great Britain, *Britain's New Citizens. The Story of the Refugees from Germany and Austria 1941–1951* (10th anniversary of AJR), London: Association of Jewish Refugees in Great Britain, 15–19.

W. Rosenstock (1956) "Exodus 1933–1939. A Survey of Jewish Emigration from Germany," *Leo Baeck Institute Year Book* I: 373–390.

M. Rosman (2009) "Jewish History across Borders," in: Jeremy Cohen and Moshe Rosman (eds.), *Rethinking European Jewish History*, Oxford: The Littman Library of Jewish Civilization, 15–29.

E. Rothschild (1972) *Meilensteine: Vom Wege der Kartell Jüdischer Verbindungen (KJV) in der Zionistischen Bewegung*, Tel Aviv: [s.n.].

J. Schloer (1995) "das Grossstadtleben nicht entbehren:" Berlin in Tel-Aviv, Grossstadtpioniere auf der Suche nach Heimat, *Exilforschung: Ein internationales Jahrbuch*, vol. 13: Claus-Dieter Krohn, Erwin Rotermund, Lutz Winckler und Wulf Köpke (Hg.): *Kulturtransfer im Exil*, Munich: Edition Text+Kritik, 166–183.

Y. Shapiro (1971) *Leadership in the American Zionist Organization*, Urbana: University of Illinois Press.

M. Shashar (1997) *Kahalom Ya'uf. Terumat Yehudei Germanya Lahayim Hadatiyim Be'eretz Yisra'el*, Jerusalem: Shashar.

P. Shatzkes (2002) *Holocaust and Rescue: Impotent or Indifferent? Anglo-Jewry 1938–1945*, New York: Palgrave.

A.J. Sherman (1973) *Island Refuge: Britain and Refugees from the Third Reich, 1933–1939*, London: P. Elek.

M. Sicron (1957) *Immigration to Israel*, Jerusalem: Falk Project for Economic Research in Israel, Central Bureau of Statistics.

W. Silberstein (1994) *My Way from Berlin to Jerusalem*, Jerusalem: [Special family edition].

M. Smith (1999) *Foley: The Spy who Saved 10,000 Jews*, London: Hodder and Stoughton.

D. Snowman (2002) *The Hitler Emigrés: The Cultural Impact on Britain of Refugees from Nazism*, London: Pimlico.

I. Sonder (2006) "Charlotte Cohn, Halutzat Ha'adrikhalut Be'eretz Yisrael,"*Zemanim* 96: 22–27.

I. Sonder (2009) *Lotte Cohn: pioneer woman architect in Israel: catalogue of buildings and projects*, Tel Aviv: Bauhaus Center.

G. Sorin (1992) *A Time for Building: The Third Immigration, 1880–1920 (The Jewish People in America,* ed. Henry Feingold vol. 3), Baltimore: Johns Hopkins University Press.

R. Stent (1980) *A Bespattered Page? The Internment of "His Majesty's Most Loyal Enemy Aliens,"* London: A. Deutsch.

R. Stent (1991) "Jewish Refugee Organizations," in: Werner Mosse (ed.), *Second Chance: Two Centuries of German-Speaking Jews in the United Kingdom*, Tübingen: J.C.B. Mohr P. Siebeck, 579–598.

L. Stone (1997) "German Zionists in Palestine before 1933," *Journal of Contemporary History* 32/2 (1997), 171–186.

H.A. Strauss (1978) "The Migration of Jews from Nazi Germany," in Herbert A. Strauss (gen. ed), *Jewish Immigrants of the Nazi Period in the USA*, vol. 1: *Archival Resources*, N.Y./Munich/ London/Paris: K. G. Saur, xiii-xxviii.

H.A. Strauss (1980–81) "Jewish Emigration from Germany: Nazi Policies and Jewish Responses," *Leo Baeck Institute Year Book*, XXV (1980): 313–361; XXVI (1981): 343–409.

H.A. Strauss (1981) *Jewish Immigrants of the Nazi Period in the USA*, 3 vols., N.Y./Munich/ London/Paris: K. G. Saur.

H.A. Strauss (1987) *Emigration deutsche Wissenschaftler nach 1933: Entlassung und Vertreibung*, Berlin: Technische Universitaet.

W. Strickhausen (1998) "Großbritannien" in: Claus-Dieter Krohn (ed.), *Handbuch der deutsch-sprahigen Emigration, 1933–1945*, Darmstadt: Primus Verlag, 251–269.

Toldot Ha'Universita (1997–2013) *Toldot Ha'Universita Ha'Ivrit BeYerushalaim*, vol. I, eds. Michael Heyd and Shaul Katz, vol. II-III, ed. Hagit Lavsky, vol. IV, ed. Assaf Selzer, Jerusalem: The Hebrew University Magnes Press.

H. Traber and E. Weingarten (1987) *Verdrängte Musik: Berliner Komponisten in Exil*, Berlin: Argon Verlag.

M. Traub (1936) *Die jüdische Auswanderung aus Deutschland: Westeuropa, Übersee, Palästina*, Berlin: Jüdische Rundschau.

A.S. Travis (2004) "From Color Makers to Chemists: A Jewish Profession Elevated," *Jahrbuch des Simon-Dubnow-Instituts* 3: 199–219.

J. Tydor Baumel (1981) "The Kitchener Transmigration Camp at Richborough,"*Yad Vashem Studies* 14: 233–246.

M. Warhaftig (2007) *They Laid the Foundations: Lives and Works of German-Speaking Jewish Architects in Palestine 1918–1948*. English translation: Andrea Lerner, Tübingen and Berlin: Wasmuth.

D.R. Weiner (2004) "The Third Wave: German Jewish Refugees Come to Baltimore," in *Lives Lost, Lives Found: Baltimore German Jewish Refugees, 1933–1945*, Baltimore, Md.: Jewish Museum of Maryland, 11–27.

L.C. White (1957) *300,000 New Americans: The Epic of a Modern Immigrant-Aid Service*, New York: Harper.

Wischnitzer (1948) *The Story of Jewish Migration since 1800*, Philadelphia: Jewish Publication Society of America.

R. Wolman (1996) *Crossing Over: An Oral History of Refugees from Hitler's Reich*, New York: Twayne Publishers.

Y. Yishai (1981) "Aliya Hadasha Vemapai: She'elat Hahaverut Hakefula," *Hatsiyonut,* 6: 241–273.

A. Zahl-Gottlieb (1998) *Men of Vision: Anglo-Jewry's Aid to Victims of the Nazi Regime, 1933–1998*, London: Weidenfeld & Nicolson.

R. Zalashik (2008) *Ad Nafesh: Mehagrim, Olim, Pelitim Vehamimsad Hapsikhiyatri Be'yisrael*, Benei Brak: Hakibbutz Hameuchad Publishing.

R. Zariz (1990) *Beriha Beterm Sho'ah: Hagiratam shel Yehudei Germanya, 1938–1941*, Lohamei Hageta'ot: Ghetto Fighters House Museum.

M. Zimmermann (2013) *Germanim neged Germanim*, Tel Aviv: Am Oved.

M. Zimmermann and Y. Hotam, eds (2006) *Bein Hamoladọt: Hayekim Bimehozoteihem*, Jerusalem: The Zalman Shazar Center.

P. Zinke (2003) *Flucht nach Palästina: Lebenswege Nürnberger Juden*, Nürnberg: ANTOGO Verlag.

B-A. Zucker (2001) *In Search of Refuge: Jews and US Consuls in Nazi Germany, 1933–1941*, London: Vallentine Mitchell.

B-A. Zucker (2010) "American Refugee Policy in the 1930s," in: Frank Caestecker and Bob Moore (eds.), *Refugees from Nazi Germany and the Liberal European States*, New York: Berghahn Books, 151–168.

Index